C000039451

Heroes
Next Door

Heroes
Next Door

by
SAMUEL JOHNSON
& HILDE HINTON

hachette
AUSTRALIA

hachette
AUSTRALIA

Published in Australia and New Zealand in 2020
by Hachette Australia
(an imprint of Hachette Australia Pty Limited)
Level 17, 207 Kent Street, Sydney NSW 2000
www.hachette.com.au

10 9 8 7 6 5 4 3 2 1

 A catalogue record for this
book is available from the
National Library of Australia

ISBN: 978 0 7336 4636 2 (hardback)

Cover and internal design by Christabella Designs
Typeset in Garamond Regular by Kirby Jones
Printed and bound in Australia by McPherson's Printing Group

 The paper this book is printed on is certified against the
Forest Stewardship Council® Standards. McPherson's
Printing Group holds FSC® chain of custody certification
SA-COC-005379. FSC® promotes environmentally
responsible, socially beneficial and economically viable
management of the world's forests.

They walk amongst us. We pass them on the streets every day. The unsung heroes in the shadows, quietly making other people's lives better when adversity strikes. Here, we shine the light on these courageous Australians. Welcome to

Heroes Next Door.

Contents

Platform One

Sharon started on the trams in Melbourne, but quickly found her calling as a train station host. Melbourne Metro, Malvern Station, Platform One.

For fourteen years, Sharon's job was to curate the best possible experience for peak-hour commuters; to help any of them in any given way, at any given time. This suited Sharon perfectly, as the job required her to simply be herself. She was a bona fide helper years before the job emerged. In the interview for the position, her passion for helping others was obvious and she was promptly hired, because you can't fake generosity of spirit.

Platform One became home for Sharon. Every morning she'd colourfully decorate her blackboard to greet incoming commuters. It always came with a quote of the day, a weather report, sometimes a drawing, a joke, or a cheerful pattern; always different. Every morning she'd post a pic of her board on social media, where she became quickly and roundly adored. She personified community and was duly lauded.

Sharon knew all her commuters on a first-name basis and they all knew hers. In the winter she'd raid the lemon trees near the station and hand them out to commuters to put in their tea if they were sniffly. She hoarded and rehomed all the lost brollies. Sharon, in her own time, put together the ultimate travel pack for foreign or interstate visitors and always had them at the ready. She was known for being of expert assistance to the elderly, infirm and disabled. She would bring in home-baked treats to share, and it became a bit fashionable. More and more commuters started bringing food to share from home. Sharon was constantly being invited to dinners and parties, and she never stopped feeling surprised at how willing her commuters were to share every intimate detail about their lives.

Then there was Michelle. She came to Platform One for ten years. Michelle was rebuilding her life after a long stint behind bars, and often needed Sharon's assistance. Sharon would sit with her, make the calls, fill out the forms, teach her how to use her phone properly.

It was the homeless people within her reach that Sharon really took a shine to, though. She created a special pack for them, which she developed with the city council, to provide every relevant touchstone available for someone in crisis. That always came with a cup of hot two-minute noodles.

Sharon was mum, to everyone on Platform One for fourteen years. These days, she's been on personal leave for far longer than she'd like, and she misses it terribly. Sharon can't wait to get back to her old ways, helping all and sundry, on Platform One. Especially those who need it the most.

'When I walk I never look down. I don't look at people's faces either. I look into their eyes. You never know what they are going through, what they've been through and what they are yet to face.'

– Sharon Vanderkaay

SJ

The Patchwork Family

Mel was always a fixer. When some of her high school friends had dealings with child protection, Mel watched on. It determined her path. She was going to study social work and help kids when she grew up. Her boyfriend was not a fixer. John was a larrikin and his skylarking got him into trouble. There was a nudie run through a park and his friends thought it would be funny to leave his clothes on the steps of the nearby police station, where he was promptly arrested. There was the time John drove a quad bike to the supermarket. He thought he was racing a man walking towards the store, the man thought he was trying to run him over. The charges were dropped. John's parents left his stuff out on the verandah; it's not like he hadn't been warned. Mel the Fixer convinced her parents that John should move in with them.

A busy few years followed. Mel worked two jobs while she studied, John started his own bricklaying business and they settled into the rundown house they had bought. Mel began working with high-risk teens and soon after, they had a baby. Before their son turned one, Mel asked John whether he'd thought about fostering kids. He most certainly had not, nor was he keen on the idea. At all. But he agreed with Mel when she said there was no harm in doing the training, so they could make an informed decision. John liked logic. When they mentioned the training to their parents at a Sunday family get-together, there was open dismay. Bringing in hapless strays could put their own baby at risk. As the next generation are prone to do, they went against their parents' wishes and proceeded to do the course anyway.

Two weeks after completion, there was a phone call. There were two boys aged eight and ten who were in a place that didn't meet their needs. Mel took the call, had nameplates made up for the two lads and set up two beds in the spare room. Just for the weekend of course. John agreed – after all, the nameplates were a welcoming gesture, and they could be removed as quickly as they were put up.

The two boys arrived with a garbage bag full of unclean and ill-fitting clothes. This saddened and outraged John, who threw the garbage bag in the bin and immediately took them shopping. So they'd have some reasonable clothing when they moved on – seventeen placements and counting. At the last house, the older boy had been threatened with a knife, and his brother had been too scared to stick up for him. John became immediately invested and when Monday came around, they told the program coordinator that there was no rush to remove the boys.

John was still adjusting to parenthood but knew innately that a one-year-old would always get the most attention in any family. As the weeks went on, he made sure the boys didn't feel left out. The grandparents had done a one-eighty upon meeting them at a Sunday afternoon family gathering, and Mel had decided they were going to be their boys. That she was their mum and that was the end of it. John went along willingly, but he didn't feel the way he thought he was supposed to. He was hands-on and did the sport runs, but his heart wasn't as present as his face.

After a few months, some negative behavioural patterns crept in. The older boy was regularly disrespectful towards Mel, and even though John knew this was because the lad had grown up surrounded by domestic violence, it upset him. The counselling didn't seem to be doing much good either. More often than not, John would go and collect him at the end of his sessions to find out he'd told the counsellor to get fucked and had skulked around the corner until it was time to be picked up. John couldn't get him to talk about anything, and both boys became agitated the week before their monthly access visits to their biological parents. Then it took a week afterwards for them to settle back in. The boys struggled through any transition, whether it was moving to a school closer to home or going from primary to secondary school, but John and Mel were by their side through all the hurdles.

When the boys hit high school, John and Mel sought a permanent care order. There was a bit of a scare when one biological parent refused to sign it, so off they went to court. John found this much more difficult than anything so far, but he applied the same even temperament and determination to succeed as he had through all their ups and downs. They got custody, and as they celebrated at their regular Sunday family get-together, John looked around at his family the way it was. The way it always would be. He didn't know when it had stopped being hard, but it had.

John decided it was time to renovate the house. He'd laid his last brick some time back and had landed a fancy government job. He almost didn't get it because that darned nudie run came up in his police check. But they took a chance on him and when he and Mel gained full custody of the boys, he was given three months parental leave. As he began to renovate, he found his knees locking. He also lost control of his foot one day as he came down the stairs. Turned out he had MS. It's primary progressive, which means any deterioration is permanent. He was recently seen on Facebook precariously rolling his mobility scooter over a big green ball. The caption read 'Audition tape for the Crusty Demons'. He's still a larrikin.

The kids are grown now. The older boy has saved three thousand dollars towards buying a house. He's an adult and is choosing not to see his biological parents at the moment. The younger boy is about to finish school and plans on being a chef. The baby they had when the boys came to stay is eleven and has never known life without his brothers. Mel has just stopped paying agistment fees for Mr Harley Davidson, the horse she got when she was twelve. John knows that they could have bought a car with those fees, but he doesn't care because he knows Mel is always in for life.

HH

Hero in Waiting

Lachie wasn't one of those kids who knew what he wanted to be when he grew up, but he hoped it involved sport. What he did know, was that he wanted to travel the world; so he worked his backside off and started saving. Two jobs – pub work a few evenings a week and a supermarket by day. Sure, he was aware that adults tell their kids they need to do well in school or they'll end up being a check-out chick. But he didn't mind that; he was going to travel the world and start coaching some junior sports teams. Got to start somewhere.

Then COVID hit. The pub job was gone, but his hours at the supermarket grew. All of a sudden he was an essential worker, and some people were thanking him. But it wasn't all roses. There were lines up the street outside the store, and a lot of people forgot their manners, their grace. They clambered over each other, snatched toilet paper and tomato paste out of each other's hands. The staff around him were being abused at every turn. Not so much in Lachie's case – he's built like a brick shithouse, sports a crew cut and his soft centre could be easily disguised with pinpoint accurate stares. He had to call the police on occasion, when it got to fisticuffs, and he never thought twice about defending his multicultural colleagues when they were spattered with racist comments on the daily. Lachie never responded loudly, or aggressively, but clearly and calmly. He maintained an even disposition amongst the chaos.

The days were long and busy and he did his best to keep an eye on the stadium-sized crowds flooding the store. He stayed away from his girlfriend – her sister had a heart transplant as a child, and he didn't want to put anyone at risk. Just before full lockdown, he would stand up the driveway, talking on the phone to his sweetheart who would wave and blow kisses from her car parked down the way.

His dreams were all in disarray too. There wouldn't be any travel for a while. There would eventually, though, so he kept saving. He wouldn't be volunteering to coach any juniors yet either. The mania died down, and people realised they didn't have to raid the shelves like they had at the start of the pandemic. Lachie even took a week off in the calm after the storm. He had a few sleep-ins, and when they asked him to come back earlier than planned, he put his hand up.

The big bosses decided the staff had gone over and above and gave them three $50 dollar vouchers each, as a gesture of thanks. His housemates were stoked when Lachie told them – their work had dried up, like so many others, and now they could do a big shop. But in the end, there were no vouchers to give. Lachie had come across three homeless people near his CBD supermarket, three amongst the many, and given them one each. There weren't enough to go round, but one fellow told him not to worry. That they'd share.

HH

Would You Send Me Back if I Was Broken?

Lilly was a bright, curious girl with no reason to be otherwise. Her mum, Tanya, warm and kind-eyed, collected broken cows. Ceramic cows with ears missing; sculpted metal cows long-rusted and all wonky and drunk looking; toy cows with missing eyes, lumpy bits and faded spots. Everyone in the family collected things. It's just how they were. Even Dad's old boots weren't thrown out. Why throw Tomsy's boots out when they could move out to the garden and be effortlessly repurposed into perfectly charming plant pots? Others saw dead boots where Mum Tanya saw new life. Mum Tanya and champ-Dad Tomsy held the philosophy that their home should provide a haven for broken things that would ordinarily be forgotten. Otherwise where would they live and who would care for them? They valued uniqueness. The weird, the wonderful and the broken.

When Lilly was just two or three she developed an obsession with Steve Irwin. Older sister Paige can, to this day, recite every word of 'The Elephants of India' song from Bindi's fitness DVD that Lilly played on maximum rotation. While other kids got swept up in Wiggle-mania, young Lilly was much more likely to be seen marching proudly up the main street showing off her massive blow-up crocodile.

Mum Tanya arranged for a friend in Queensland to visit Australia Zoo and buy a Steve Irwin teddy from the souvenir shop, then send it down to them. Lilly loved her Steve Irwin teddy more than anything. After a while, the stitching on her teddy's hands came undone and fluff started falling out. Lilly was concerned enough about the health of her teddy to prompt Mum Tanya to call Australia Zoo and ask for a replacement to be sent. The folk at Australia Zoo asked them to return the injured teddy and promised to send a new one. Lilly wasn't appeased; in fact, she grew more upset. Later that night, while she was being tucked in all snug, she looked up and asked her mum.

'Would you send me back if I was broken?'

Mum Tanya promised Lilly they wouldn't send her teddy with sore hands anywhere, reminded Lilly of all the broken cows, and explained that in their house, broken things could stay as long as they wanted and would always be loved.

The following morning, Mum Tanya rang the souvenir shop and explained that returning the teddy with broken hands was no longer possible. The lady on the phone at Australia Zoo told her to keep the teddy and that they'd already sent the replacement. When Mum Tanya tried to pay for the extra teddy, the lady laughed and told her not to worry about it because 'Steve wouldn't mind'.

Not long after, Steve Irwin died suddenly. Lilly was shattered by the news and mourned his death more acutely than most. She learnt then, at a very impressionable age, that heroes can die, that heroes are human, and that no one is immune to the vicissitudes of Father Time. To honour her love for the Irwin family, Lilly solemnly made the decision to dress as Bindi, in solidarity. Out came the khaki. Bindi-style pigtails became a permanent fixture. Lilly dressed as Bindi Irwin for two years before deciding she had appropriately honoured the Irwin family.

* * *

By school age, Lilly, her sister, Paige, and brother, Aarron, would return from school camps and every time, without fail, Mum Tanya would be waiting eagerly with a cluster of friends and rellies, waving a welcome home poster, crying her eyes out. Their very own love parade.

Growing up, Lilly became a huge fan of the famed thoroughbred Black Caviar and, for a time, proudly sported pyjamas that exactly matched Black Caviar's race colours. She loved collecting information as well, to bolster her collections. Lilly went through a Test Cricket phase and would keep meticulous stats sheets from every Test match she watched before carefully marking the pertinent stats on her variously collected player posters.

Lilly and Paige adopted their champ-Dad Tomsy's habit of purchasing the most limp and forlorn plants from the supermarket, knowing that once in Mum Tanya's hands, they would be lovingly restored to robustness.

When she became old enough to go to concerts with sister Paige, Lilly started collecting rip-off concert t-shirts from the weird guy selling them outside the stadium. There was always a weird guy outside the stadium hawking imitation concert shirts, and Lilly always preferred to support those guys because they were unique. Her ticket price already went to the band or group she was seeing; this way, more people came out on top and she could collect the unique memorabilia 'true fans' *didn't* collect!

Lilly's most prized collection, though, was undoubtedly her wrapping paper collection, which she felt *very* sentimental towards. Lilly would unwrap each gift she received as fastidiously as an archaeologist on a dig, to preserve the integrity of the wrapping paper; that way she could extract from it a perfect, uncreased sample from each papered prezzie, to commemorate each act of giving. Over the years, her dedication to her wrapping paper collection was thoroughly questioned, but every time she was quizzed she would invariably state who gave what to whom and when. She knew intimately the history of each parchment. Lilly was as familiar with her wrapping paper as Mum Tanya was of her cows' various misfortunes.

By the age of fourteen, Lilly was living the fullest possible life. She belonged to three different netball teams, was taking up windsurfing and riding in HPV events (those bikes you pedal from the lying position). She was freely pursuing her interests without care for what others thought and was developing into an impressive, independent, unique human with a stubborn streak. She wasn't backwards in coming forwards. Despite being the youngest, she became the trusted go-to for sister Paige and brother Aarron. Lilly worked as hard to keep the family together as her mum Tanya did, at the behest of no one, providing a critical ballast during the family's most perilous times. Mum Tanya can't imagine where the family unit would've ended up if not for Lilly's fortitude and seemingly boundless positivity.

After traversing another family crisis with graceful maturity, Lilly started going to bed straight after school. This wasn't standard teenage lethargy; it was entirely uncharacteristic. Mum Tanya sensed something serious was afoot.

Fourteen-year-old Lilly was taken to the city, diagnosed with leukemia at the Royal Children's Hospital and thrust immediately into treatment. Some people choose to dwell in their disasters. Not Lilly. She would remain the funky, kinda goofy girl she always was; the only thing that changed was her sudden cravings for battered savs. Lilly even ended up with a picture of a battered sav she found on Google as the wallpaper on her phone. Champ-Dad Tomsy, who wasn't much a fan of the big smoke, would often be sent on random missions to find the best battered sav in Melbourne.

There was a little boy, much younger than Lilly, undergoing treatment in the same ward. He'd ride his tiny pushbike around the ward each day. He was allowed to on the proviso that he took good care, and the little fella took heed – not wanting to be deprived of his riding privileges. He always looked out for Lilly and no matter how much pain she was in, or how weak she became, she'd always muster a smile as he rode past. Often he'd stop and they'd chat. They became very good buddies indeed.

Lilly wasn't much for the whole status thing. She'd wilfully interrupt important bedside chats with doctors and nurses to make a point of thanking the cleaner, Doris, by name. She smiled through it all – sure, she had shitty days, but she laughed them off with her 'Little Box of Fucks' cards, which she bought from her favourite cancer charity. She always found a path to laughter. It's what made her Lilly.

'One day closer to home', became one of her most favoured expressions and, sure enough, after ten harrowing months of rigorous treatments, after becoming a quadriplegic and losing all functionality, Lilly ended up home. Gone at fifteen years and six days.

Her room remains unchanged, her collections still intact, including her beloved wrapping paper collection. Her blow-up crocodile lies airless, but a photo of Lilly with her croc and her siblings is still up on the wall. Her rip-off concert t-shirts from the weird guys outside the stadium. Her Test Cricket posters, pertinent stats still marked. Her Black Caviar PJs. Her Steve Irwin teddy, and its replacement. They're all still there.

Champ-Dad Tomsy, Mum Tanya, sister Paige and brother Aarron miss their little girl. And each day without her is now, for them, one day closer to home.

SJ

Christmas Cactus

The doorbell doesn't often ring when you're not expecting someone, especially at night. Cynthia padded down the hallway to see who was at the door in late May 1998. There was a very short, somewhat dowdy, woman standing on the doorstep. Her little round face smiled up at Cynthia as she held out a purple orchid. Turns out her name was Carol, she lived in the neighbourhood and just wanted to give Cynthia and her family a wee plant as a way of acknowledging their recent loss. Cynthia and husband Darryl were polite folk, and invited Carol inside – despite it all being a bit awkward. After some small talk, Carol took her leave. Cynthia placed the plant on the patio and didn't think twice about her neighbour from down the way.

Cynthia and Darryl had lost their five-year-old daughter, Brianna, earlier that month after a two-year battle with leukemia. Towards the end of Brianna's life, the family took her home, so she could die surrounded by family and love. It had its difficulties, though. No matter how many times Cynthia would ask relatives not to come over without ringing first, the doorbell would sound. And then there were all those 'helpful' people suggesting vitamin C injections, religious ceremonies and reminding the family that there was always hope – when there wasn't any. Cynthia understood that people don't know what to say and dug deep to find her grace during those last weeks. For Cynthia, Darryl and little sister Kayla, it was about Brianna, so they ignored the comments and goings-on as best they could.

When Brianna died, her four-year-old sister said leukemia was like broccoli. When asked what she meant, little Kayla said because it's always there, hiding behind the trees, just like broccoli.

Carol knocked on the door in late May for years to come, and each time she presented the family with a new plant in memory of Brianna, from a weeping fig to a Christmas cactus. Never on the anniversary of Brianna's death, but always in the same month. One year, Carol brought over a maidenhair fern and got to pat the new baby on the head. A boy who would never know his sister. Cynthia and Carol got to know each other quite well; turns out Carol can talk the leg off an iron pot, and Cynthia looked forward to answering the doorbell of an evening each May. 'That'll be Carol,' she'd say as she padded down the hallway each time.

When little Kayla was sixteen, Cynthia took her to a doctor who said 'you're one pissed off young lady' when she walked in the door. Well, Kayla just broke. Cynthia and Darryl had kept open lines of communication about Brianna's death, but Kayla harboured immense secret guilt – even though she was only four when her sister died. Four-year-old Kayla didn't know the specifics, but she knew she was going to hospital to help her sister. And she believed that when she woke up, her bone marrow would have made her big sister better. But she wasn't better, and Kayla thought it was all her fault. All those years she had harboured this pain and Cynthia couldn't believe she hadn't noticed. That huge half-hour long cry sure helped though. It was cathartic for Kayla, and her folks were able to deal with the problem now they could see it. That year when Carol rang the doorbell, she presented the family with daffodil bulbs. Cynthia planted them, the right way up and everything, but the bulbs never took.

This year was the twenty-second year in a row that Carol has rung that doorbell and stood there with a plant for the family. It's the smallest of gestures, but for Cynthia, it shows someone is with her in her grief. That she's not alone. It's more than a plant, it's an unspoken, consistent and unwavering acknowledgement of what the family have been through. Like friendships, there are only a handful of surviving plants. But that Christmas cactus sure has grown like the clappers. It has a solid trunk and sprouts beautiful pink and white flowers that light up the patio once a year. Just like Carol.

HH

No Diamonds
for This Girl

Carboor is a tiny little post–World War I town with a memorial hall, a church that hasn't been used in donkey's and a pub that's been a pile of bricks since the fifties. All that's really left in the valley is a canoe factory and cows. There is, of course, your typical array of gun-loving farmers. And then there's Kylie and Maisie.

Kylie is proud chieftain of four dogs and a husband who resorts to regular golfing, Pete. Kylie's dogs comprise of Emmy, her Staffy cross (a fierce little rodent hunter); Pepper, her German Shepherd (hard working, loves the camera); Junior, her old male Staffy (daft old bugger, demented); and Bert, son of Pepper (huge brown doofus). Together, Kylie, Pete and the four dogs share a little loft house on a couple of acres, a stone's throw from Carboor. Over the years, Kylie has harboured an extraordinary number of different animals on the property – from poultry, sheep and horses, to parrots, fish and reptiles – but she has toned down on the whole Dr Dolittle thing over recent years, in part to keep hubby's golfing habit in check, and in part to allow space for their shared love of permaculture.

Kylie, a self-confessed 'army brat', had her fate sealed the day she was born, when her dad celebrated her birth by getting his newborn daughter a dingo cross, bred out on the boondocks at Ipswich. Growing up, Kylie's dad would move koalas off the road to safety, and before long, he was bringing illicit animals home, and making sure Kylie didn't tell Mum. One time they housed some cockatoos in the shed for three months before Mum caught wind. Needless to say, Kylie's youth was peppered with animals, horses. motorbikes and sweet freedom.

In 2000, Kylie's dad ended his life – Kylie still has words with him about that one. She thanks her father for her love of animals though, for with it came a depth of understanding that led her to do extensive work with assistance animals helping veterans with PTSD. Because of this, Kylie feels her dad's death wasn't totally in vain.

Kylie had lived in her loft house in Carboor for less than a year when she first encountered Maisie. After discovering an injured joey on the roadside, Kylie asked around for the local wildlife carer. She was directed towards the 'crazy kangaroo lady', who happened to live just a couple of Ks from Kylie's loft house/menagerie.

After passing Enders Lane to get home countless times, Kylie finally drove down it, with the injured joey in her car, and felt immediately like she had stepped back in time. After the cattle grid, she passed through gorgeous paddocks, to another set of gates, beyond which lay an abundant dam on the left, leading to a land bridge curbed by a thriving swamp, opening out into Maisie's garden proper, a blaze of colour, smothered in magic.

Maisie was, of course, found outside in the garden upon Kylie's arrival. She could be seen, as she is to this day, with some old beanie jammed over her head, wearing her late husband Stan's cardigan, wet-weather pants and medium-length gumboots. (She's seventy-four and can't remove full-sized gumboots anymore, so she opts for medium-length and removes them by hooking the back of the boot on the leg of her kitchen chair.) Maisie stood at around pixie height and was shy, but an engaging twinkle shone through her reticence. Maisie directed Kylie and her injured joey inside, past a cockatoo manning the gate, and as soon as Maisie referred to her cockatoo as 'a savage little fiend', Kylie knew she loved Maisie. Their friendship was sealed before Kylie walked through the front door.

Maisie carries a walking stick now, and rescued joeys, birds and wombats still recover at her feet in her sculpted wonderland. Maisie likes her wombats the most, because they're feisty and bratty. But she was pretty keen on her emu too, who stayed with her for twenty-eight years before passing away recently.

When Kylie moved to town with her Dolittle leanings, Maisie was just the 'crazy kangaroo lady'. But years have passed. Bread has been broken. And many of the gun-loving farmers in the region use their guns more judiciously now, and often ferry injured livestock and animals over to Maisie's vivid garden of plenty, where they know the animals will be cared for until they're well enough to choose whether to go or stay.

SJ

Back From Nowhere

From her very first sip of alcohol at sixteen, Emma was hooked. She had never been comfortable in her own skin. She was socially awkward; an escapist. Alcohol made it all go away. It was an elixir. She could smile; she was interesting, confident, able. Before long, she left home and was a functioning alcoholic who ploughed her way through VCE and almost finished her social welfare course at university. But in the last stages of placement, she told herself she couldn't help anyone. If she couldn't run her own life, surely she would ruin others. So she quit her studies.

Emma found a partner with similar interests and they drank for the next ten years. And drank. And drank.

They complemented each other's neuroses beautifully. During this time, they tried to have a family. She was desperate for children. Being pregnant would fix everything. It would stop her drinking. It would make her well. When she finally fell pregnant, she was surprised to find that she wasn't better after all. She muddled through parenting as best she could. Photos of Emma from this time show a woman struggling to hold her eyelids open; visible trepidation, deep sadness, stooped shoulders. Her relationship broke down.

When her daughter was seven, Emma had a particularly big night on the booze. She doesn't recall making any conscious decisions to suicide, but she took every pill she could find in the house. There were many.

Her young daughter loved school more than anything else, and if there was no school excursion the following morning, Emma knows that the outcome would have been different. It's not like her daughter had never seen Mum passed out on the couch before. Normally she would have made her own breakfast and taken herself off to school, but *this* morning there was an excursion and she had to wake up her mum so she could sign the permission form or she wouldn't be able to go. She shook her mother over and over, trying to rouse her. When she couldn't, the young girl called an ambulance, and Emma lives to tell her tale.

The following Mother's Day was spent in a psych hospital, with her daughter in the care of DHS. The girl was lucky there was a kinship care option and she moved in with her paternal grandparents. On this Mother's Day in the psych ward, Emma was watching TV in the leisure room. There was a fellow, who had unicycled around the country to raise money for cancer research, handing over a cheque. He spoke of a promise he had made to his sister. Emma watched on thinking that there were people out there getting on with things. Doing things for others. Not like her. She was choosing to bathe in her own trauma. She concluded that she needed to do something. Anything. She eliminated riding a unicycle (she's most uncoordinated). But maybe, she thought, she could contact her family? Maybe she could make some promises herself? So, she rang her parents, her sisters, and the message was clear. They all implored her to go to rehab.

It was a slow road up. Her first rehab didn't take. Neither did the next. Emma says everything has to align for rehab to work. The right program, the right psych, the right state of being within oneself. At Odyssey she edged forward. She got what she needed from her treatment at the right time. She had been in therapy on and off since she was fourteen. But it was attendance rather than participation. After a few tries, she found the sweet spot. She began unpacking and analysing her self-harm episodes.

She hadn't known how to feel anything sober. And after a while she couldn't feel anything drunk. Self-harm proved that she existed – to herself. At least she felt something. She had been so unbelievably afraid, lost, trapped. But she persisted with her programs. She was diagnosed with an official condition, which she saw as a label. But having a label gave her ownership. She was provided a trauma-based psychologist and dug deep into her fears.

Slowly, slowly she hauled herself out of the quicksand. She worked on her relationship with her daughter, with the grandparents, with DHS. She realised she could help others, which was her intention all those years ago when she studied social welfare. And she is well on the way. She's back at uni and dreams of working in program development. She has seen the gaps herself. If she hadn't been savvy, she would have cut her losses with her daughter and moved on, as many other parents do. She admits there are children who need to be in permanent care, but there are plenty of parents who get better and should be aiming for family reunification.

Emma's daughter is finishing primary school this year, and she will remain with her grandparents until then. Emma wants her to graduate with her friends. By Christmas, though, Emma will have been two years sober. She has navigated DHS and the courts and has been issued a family reunification order. Her girl is coming home. Emma admits her daughter's experiences aren't what any young girl should have to go through, but she accepts that they happened and maintains an honest narrative with her now tweenager. And because her mother has always kept open and honest lines of communication, Emma's daughter is excited about the next phase of their lives.

Emma donates to Love Your Sister even though she has never been touched by cancer. Nor has her family. She credits Love Your Sister for providing a sense of community; inspiration. We credit her for fighting her tush off. For not taking the easy road. Welcome back, Emma.

HH

The Little Teacher
Who Could

John was dressed in a flying possum costume when he first clapped eyes on the love of his life, Sandy. He asked her out backstage on opening night. She made him wait until the end of the show before saying yes. Sure, he was a ham, but his unabashed, fun-loving nature obscured a true heart. Sandy knew that John wouldn't give her the run-around. This goose dressed as a possum, known affectionately as John, was cooked from the get-go.

John was a do-anything type of fella. Marathon? Easy done. Deep sea exploration with the Northern Territory

Museum to find the anchors of the HMS *Beagle*? No drama. Ride a camel from Katherine to Tennant Creek? Sounds like a hoot. John was a dashing, wholesome bloke with a slightly bent nose, blonde hair and blue eyes, standing a pinch over six foot tall. He'd have been quite the catch if Sandy wasn't such a prospect herself.

Marriage was never in question and the two promptly tied the knot, sharing a dream of raising four kids together. Soon after they wed, Sandy joined John in Tennant Creek, where he had taken a placement as a copper for the Northern Territory Police. Tennant Creek in 1983 was heat, dust and flies. In varying orders. Real outback. Back then it had two general stores and that was about it. At first glance.

All you have when you're so far away from everything, in such a harsh environment, is each other, and Sandy and John settled into the community perfectly. Unlike other towns, where you could feel observed or judged, Tennant Creek was progressive for its time. Once you were there, you were part of their melting pot, no questions asked. There was one local man in particular who loved getting around town in a frock, and two hoots weren't given. You could be whoever you wanted to be in Tennant Creek in 1983.

Adventure abounded for this willing young couple. Sandy graduated from teacher's college and was given her first placement at Ali Curung, a tiny Aboriginal settlement in the middle of nowhere. When Sandy arrived, she was put in charge of the 'Junior Nomads', a cluster of five- to eight-year-olds who specialised in truancy. Over the previous school holidays someone had locked a dangerous dog in Sandy's allotted portable classroom, so it was a 'start from scratch' kind of deal. First thing for Sandy to do was to make the classroom habitable. Second thing for Sandy was to work out how to keep these little pocket rockets at school.

Sandy switched it up. She instituted 'shower time' in the morning (there was a shower block at the school), then she started stretching out breakfast time, by a little more each day. Sandy created a more interactive curriculum, with a more experiential approach, to counter the tediousness of worksheet learning. She was a carer too, which is fundamentally why her kids loved her. Sandy wasn't judgy, and she cared. That works everywhere. Before long, the kids were happy to stay all day long, and their nickname 'Junior Nomads' became a thing of the past.

Meanwhile, John left his police cadetship, wondering whether policing was for him. During his existential crisis, John got a job in a factory, before being fired after being found asleep on the toilet. One of his mates resigned in solidarity the same day. While Sandy fell straight into the groove of teaching, it's safe to say that John was still finding his feet.

The lovebirds ended up nesting in Katherine after John eventually finished his police cadetship and earnt his first post. There, Sandy began her career as a remote teacher for the Katherine School of the Air, teaching over the radio airwaves to kids all across the Northern Territory who lived remotely, on cattle stations and such. Their homework would be sent out and back by snail mail – no computers back then. When Sandy wasn't on the radio, she was flying all about the Northern Territory visiting her students who lived days from everywhere. These were good times. Sandy was flying high and John was becoming quite the community copper. The type of copper who wouldn't book you for speeding if you were a few Ks over the limit; however, if you'd been speeding *and* had your kids in the car, well that was a different story. John also did a lot of work with local youths, through the schools. It meant a lot to him. The other coppers soon started telling him he was too nice to be a copper. Time would tell.

Outside of work, John and Sandy were wholesome community types. Social butterfly that he was, John shone everywhere, be it at the squash courts, the cricket pitch, or the bowling green. Sandy would make chocolates for kids' birthday parties down at the local pharmacy with her friend Ronnie, and visit friends for cuppas. She'd hold Trivial Pursuit parties. Friends started making jokes about the couple. They'd say that if John and Sandy broke up they'd know the world was ending. Something would really be wrong then!

After seven years of adventure, learning and growing together, it became time for Sandy and John to punch out some kidlets. Four was still the aim.

On 4 June 1987 their firstborn entered the world. Bradley. Their boy so true. After an uneventful first two days in the world, Bradley started fitting and was airlifted with Sandy to a hospital in Darwin. There it was concluded that these were infant seizures, and that Bradley would grow out of them. Not to be. Bradley continued to have seizures and surgeries. An MRI at four years of age revealed lesions on his brain. He had epilepsy and would need medication to control the seizures for the rest of his life. Around this time Bradley lost all speech. Sandy and John worked tirelessly to get him talking again, not knowing at the time just how many 'Bradleyisms' would eventuate.

By the time Bradley was five years and nine months old he had three younger brothers who adored him – as planned, he was indeed one of four children to Sandy and John. Bradley's brothers didn't adore him because he was disabled. They adored him for who he was. Bradley was a true gem of a person. He was most gentle and his heart beat unique and pure. Bradley was extremely sensitive to injustice and it was almost as if he could literally feel other people's pain. Coupled with his next-level empathy, Bradley maintained the most calibrated moral compass imaginable. His empathic nature and virtuous moral code incidentally provided his brothers with the perfect benchmark to work off.

By the time Bradley was eight he was diagnosed with high-functioning autism. By the age of eleven it was discovered that Bradley had mild cerebral palsy. Although he was the big brother, he became the little brother to his brothers, who took care of him and protected him constantly, without question. Life wasn't easy for Bradley, but Sandy and John upheld their mantra – it is what it is, make allowances, not excuses. Hold every boy equally to account.

In between Little Athletics, piano lessons, Joeys and Scouts, St John's Cadets, acting and drawing classes, and cross-country running, dad John developed a kidney problem. His kidney was bung and by the time his kids were grown he'd need a new one. Sandy offered hers of course. Then he'd really be stuck with her.

2016

Bradley is staying in his own sleep-out, which he loves, while his three brothers one by one begin to move out of home. Bradley spends his days learning binary code and computer programming and teaching himself Latin. Second brother, Justin, leaves home and starts studying science at the National University in Canberra, supporting himself with a side-gig at JB Hi-Fi. Third brother, Simon, falls into love and family, and moves twenty minutes away from the family home and Bradley, who becomes the most doting uncle ever when Simon fathers two girls. Fourth and youngest brother, Shane, loves to study and has completed his Masters. Shane was eligible for Mensa by the age of seven, but Sandy decided not to enrol him. Shane is clearly having the last laugh with each unit he completes. He loves out-schooling the little teacher who could. The teacher they all call Mum.

4 June

Sandy, John, Bradley and the brothers all get together for Bradley's twenty-ninth birthday. A fine time is had over his favourite dinner – steak, eggs, chips and baked beans. Sandy makes Bradley a Malteser cake which is too rich for even his sweet tooth. It is a crackerjack affair, with merriment aplenty.

20 July

Sandy is woken at 4 a.m. by Bradley, coming in from his sleep-out. This is normal. Nature is calling. As he plods back to his room, Sandy asks from her bed as he passes if he is okay. He replies 'I'm okay' and Sandy tells him to try to get some sleep. Sandy is wide awake by now, so she shuffles to the kitchen, fixes herself a cuppa and sips her way towards the day that beckons.

Sandy's son Simon is dropping off their eldest granddaughter at 8 a.m. when Sandy realises that Bradley hasn't come in for his morning medication yet. She goes to his sleep-out to check on him. As soon as she opens the door she knows something is wrong. No Bradley jumping up and saying he is coming in. Sandy screams. John and Simon come running. Someone calls triple zero. The other sons rush over, or hurriedly book flights. Numbness. Shock. Statements to police. Watching their beautiful boy being wheeled away. So many tears. So much pain.

Sandy's beautiful boy so true, Bradley, is pronounced dead, aged twenty-nine. Cause of death: SUDEP – sudden unexpected death in epilepsy.

The inevitable flurry of urgent phone calls. Flowers. Cards. Condolences. Organising a funeral they don't want. Delays because of the coroner and the autopsy. Simon writes and sings a song for his brother at the service. John delivers a lovely, difficult eulogy. Brothers Simon and Justin speak honourably of their big-little brother. They hold a dance party to open the funeral, to Bradley's favourite song, 'Good Times', by Carly Rae Jepsen.

Now

Sandy lives without her little boy so true. Her little compass might be gone, but Sandy is keeping Bradley's spirit alive and well. Sandy now works as a disability carer in a house with four men. 'Sandy' in Greek means 'carer of men'. Sandy has been caring for her four disabled fellas for nearly three years now. They're non-verbal but there's plenty going on upstairs. One of her blokes has a wicked sense of humour and laughs his head off every day at this, that or the other. It's a happy house, just like Sandy's. The four men are ageing, have been in the house since 1989, and their parents are now either very elderly or passed, so Sandy is a vital part of their lives, valued dearly because she treats them as she knows their mums would want them treated.

Sandy is trying to care for the person, not the disability, as she's always done. She's doing what she knows worked best for Bradley. The same thing that worked best for her Junior Nomads, years before Bradley was born. She's not judgy and she cares. That works everywhere.

Back home, with all their boys now having flown the coop, Sandy and John are as happy with their life as they've always been, describing it as 'comfy, like a pair of slippers'. John enjoys his woodwork in the shed and Sandy is currently cross-stitching a massive picture of Bradley with his two nieces. Sandy and John finish each other's sentences and they still give each other as good as they get. Peas in a comfy little pod.

Every year without fail, when 4 June rolls around, no matter where in the world the family all may be, they each cook up Bradley's favourite meal – steak, eggs, chips and baked beans – and they raise an iced coffee to their beloved little genius who taught them all to love harder and care better.

Then it's straight back to looking after her various fellas, for our little teacher who could, Sandy, Carer of Men.

SJ

Stefanie's Wish

Young Stefanie was a prankster, a sneak, who specialised in wet willies. Any car trip was long if she was sitting behind you. But she was also fiercely protective of her sister and friends. Older Stefanie had a stellar work ethic and always thought of others. One day, she was in the car with her dad when a motorcycle pulled up alongside them. She mentioned that her boyfriend was thinking of getting one, and her dad, Tom, said riders were organ donors in waiting. This opened the door for her to tell Tom that she was already on the organ donor register and that if anything was to happen to her, it was her wish that she give someone out there the ultimate gift. And perhaps he should consider doing the same.

When Stefanie was twenty-four, she turned up at Tom's work to get a lift home – they enjoyed their one-on-one time in the car. While chatting away with one of Tom's colleagues as she waited for him, Stefanie stopped mid-sentence and collapsed. Luckily Tom's workplace made sure the staff were first aiders, and they performed CPR while they waited for the ambulance. Tom was distraught as he sat in the ambulance with his daughter. His workmates knew his wife, Linda, was away taking care of her father, and by the time he arrived at the hospital, they had arranged to fly her home.

It was an inexplicable brain aneurysm, and Stefanie didn't make it. But the CPR had helped, and her mum got to the hospital in time to hold Stefanie's hand through those last precious days. Stefanie was able to help five people with organ transplants and two people with her tissue. A lady received a combined kidney and pancreas transplant, another lady got a heart. There's a man out there with both her lungs, a woman with her other kidney, and a sick young girl got her liver. Two people can now see thanks to corneal transplants.

When you register as an organ and tissue donor, the family left behind still have to sign off for the donation to occur. Stefanie's family knew that if there was a possibility that she could give the gift of a healthier life to others, that it would be her wish. None of the family thought twice. There are limited circumstances that allow medical teams to perform the required surgery and to then get the organs to another team for the recipients, and the whole family is proud that Stefanie got her wish to save lives should the worst ever happen.

Tom and Linda are now community champions for organ donation and they proudly represent DonateLife at community events. They don't shy away from difficult conversations, and they let anyone who'll listen know that nine out of ten families go ahead with organ donation when their loved ones are on the register, but it drops to six out of ten if the family doesn't know that their loved one wanted to donate.

For Tom, it's about increasing available organs. He encourages registration and reminds people to talk about it with all and sundry in their lives. He always opens any conversation on organ donation with the same question: 'Would you like organs to be available should anything happen to you or your loved ones?'

HH

Gail Force

When people get sick, the lucky ones have a nucleus of people around them all the time. The close people who do the hospital sits, hold hands, get ice chips while waiting for surgery. They collect those little things that mean a lot, like the right pyjamas or pillow, and run around sorting out the life stuff, from picking up kids, cooking and washing to those pesky day-to-day errands that don't stop just because someone is ill or incapacitated. That's where Cara sat when her sister, Manda, got real sick, real quick.

Manda had been with her partner, John, for over ten years and they had never got around to getting married, even though they'd always wanted to. A terminal diagnosis accelerated their wedding dream to the top of their to-do list, and Cara took on the job. She was dropping her kids off at school in a haze of stress one day when Gail, another mother she had seen around, asked Cara how things were going. It's not uncommon for a light question from a stranger to bring out a geyser of emotions, to open the floodgates, to break us down, and Cara let fly with the tale of her sick sister who wanted to get married before she died. Gail immediately kicked into gear for this virtual stranger.

The first thing Gail did was arrange a morning tea to raise medicine money for the family. Cara was so grateful because she wasn't able to organise her way out of a paper bag while she sat in the nucleus trying to help as much as she could. All her organisational skills had left the building when her dear sister got sick, and watching Gail do her thing was inspiring. Medicine money, check. Time to figure out a wedding. Cara explained it would be a small affair, there wasn't much money, and Gail asked, if she wouldn't mind, whether she could take the reins on the wedding – with Cara as chief advisor. Cara didn't mind at all.

Gail harnessed the locals, cold-called half of Victoria, and before you could say 'Manda's wedding day', it was Manda's wedding day. The town had got together and decorated the streets between the family home, the hall and a beautiful spot down by the local creek where the ceremony was to be held. The path down into the valley was decorated with signs and the view out onto the golden fields was idyllic. Strangers dropped off food and Gail whipped her volunteer troops into action. The makeup lady from way up on the other side of Melbourne was sent to Manda, as was the hairdresser from up the Hume. The cake from Koo Wee Rup waited proudly in the hall, surrounded by the cups and saucers from Torquay. Gail sat donated air fares at the bride and groom's table amongst the flowers; Manda and John would be off to Queensland after the ceremony for their honeymoon, and the photographer from Knox was given a tour of what, when and how by Gail betwixt and between.

The wedding from everywhere was ready. Manda made her way from her palliative care unit down through the decorated streets, stood beside the flowing creek amongst golden fields and married her sweetheart. There wasn't a dry eye to be seen, but everyone smiled and cheered. They ate and drank and reminisced their way through the reception and waved the happy couple off to their honeymoon. Their friends, who now included Gail, had rallied and done all these amazing things; things that those in the nucleus rarely have the capacity to do. The pretty things, the icing on the cake. The things that make being in the nucleus bearable. Manda chose not to return to the palliative care unit on her return; she chose to die at home surrounded by family and photos from her big day.

Gail just loves doing things for strangers. Not just for Manda and Cara. Each Christmas she gathers gifts for struggling families – she threw together a gingerbread baking day to raise funds to fly a dying man's son over from Perth and she organises balls to not only fundraise, but to bring people together. This has led those who attend Gail's events to realise they can do the same. Her goodwill and can-do attitude has led to other Gails popping up around the place. Perhaps we could all look a bit deeper – to our inner Gail. That bit that gives us the courage to reach out to a stranger. To do something.

HH

Doomsday Dash

Looking at it, you might just think of it as some big old box. To Jessa it means so much more. In fact, it is a ballast box of significant historical importance from the Second Fleet. There were two boxes. They were passed down to Jessa's grandfather, who left Jessa's mum and her uncle one box each in his will. The will stipulated that the two children choose a box each, without inspecting the contents – whatever was inside was theirs! Jessa's mum's chosen box contained antique sheet music and a beautiful ebony and silver clarinet. That big ballast box became home to the family's most significant keepsakes as time passed. When

Jessa became a mother for the first time, her mum handed down the big ballast box to her.

On top of the original inherited items, like 1800s Gold Mine Shares, Cobb and Co. ticket stubs and a genuine flag from the 1956 Melbourne Olympics, lie Jessa's mum's keepsakes: christening candles and ticket stubs from David Bowie and Pink Floyd concerts. Now, Jessa has continued the keepsake tradition and on top of her mum's items lie new family photos, another generation of sterling silver napkin rings, and all three pregnancy tests!

Jessa's mum was a housing commission kid, adopted, and faced her share of challenges through her life. But despite, or even perhaps because of that adversity, she became a nurse and created a fulfilling life for herself and Jessa, with little to no support from 'the father'.

Jessa had a pretty tough run of it herself, but her mum was hardy and extraordinary, and she insisted on getting on with things no matter what. Jessa's third baby, a little boy, was born prematurely and was kept in hospital for ten days before being allowed home. Jessa arrived home post-birth to find the father of her three children gone. He couldn't hack it. So it was. Jessa would do the heavy lifting in the family, just as her own mum had.

Jessa's primary aim was to be the best mum in the world for her three kids, and that left no room for dwelling. Simple as that. If she dwelled on all the knocks, her kids wouldn't have the best mum in the world. So she banned bullshit. She banned regrets and self-pity. She knew it was up to her. She knew she had to take control.

* * *

New Year's Eve eve ... Bushfires had been raging around Jessa's district for weeks. The mainstream media was focused almost entirely on the fires, rolling coverage around the clock. Everyone in the district was on tenterhooks. Summer means something different for those who live outside major cities. Out where Jessa lives, summer can wipe out your family if you're not careful.

Jessa was paying strict attention to everything of course, she had been for weeks and weeks. She updated her home and contents insurance. She did what she could to make her property less vulnerable. She joined all of the community awareness groups. Jessa took her daughter Phea, aged four, to Woolies and bought $1000 worth of non-perishables like muesli bars, and they delivered them together to the Rural Fire Service. Jessa explained to little Phea that the food was for the heroes. The heroes who risked their own lives to save others. Four-year-old Phea understood clearly, and quickly became an astute hero-spotter. Phea knew all the different uniforms. She knew the RFS stood for the heroes that help people in hot danger.

On this New Year's Eve eve, the fires were way too close to Jessa's town and evacuation was the only topic on the lips of everyone in the community. At 1 a.m. Jessa woke up bolt upright. Her gut was raging. She checked the RFS site and then rang her mum, who was working a nursing night shift, hundreds of Ks away in Orange. Knowing her mum would be up all night, Jessa rang and asked her to check the RFS site hourly and ring her if anything changed before dawn. Eventually, Jessa got back to sleep.

As always, her gut beat true. At the crack of dawn the phone rang. It was Jessa's mum and she told Jessa to get out immediately. It was no longer safe and she needed to try to beat the inevitable exodus. Jessa snapped into gear. Her kids, who by Jessa's own admission can be a handful, behaved perfectly. They sensed the significance of the danger from their mum as they were woken and it was all reinforced very starkly when they looked out of the windows and saw an alien sky. Leaves and ash flew everywhere through the vivid orange. Jessa concedes she was 'shitting bricks', but that was just on the inside of course, because it was time to be Mum.

Evacuating three kids under four on your own entails a fair bit of scurrying around. The problem was the box. The big old ballast box full of keepsakes. Generations of precious keepsakes. Even after abandoning half the keepsakes, it was still too heavy. But emergencies can produce superhuman strength and Jessa somehow slid the box outside and up into the back of her car. She slammed the boot after a solid hustle, jumped into the driver's seat and started the car. As she put the car into drive, little Phea congratulated her mummy for being so strong with the memory box.

As Jessa drove away she saw walls of fire roaring over the nearest hills. It was terrifying. The thing she remembers the most distinctly, though, is the number of fire trucks headed in the opposite direction, towards the flames. She reckons she counted at least thirty.

The next twelve hours were quite the ordeal for Jessa. Plans changed, routes altered, her moods swelled, and the kids behaved *perfectly*. Jessa held on and didn't go to the toilet for the entire trip. Finally, she made it to her friend's farm, where the kids would have space and be safe from all the fires.

Jessa got out of the car and beelined for the house, straight past her concerned friend.

'Number one, I need the toilet. Number two, pour me a fucking Scotch.'

The kids were exhausted and went straight off to sleep. Jessa stayed up on her friend's verandah, drink in hand. Her bestie back home was still there as a frontline worker.

Jessa rang and asked her to check on her home. Jessa's gut told her the house didn't survive and once again her gut beat true. It was all gone.

Despite going a little numb, Jessa didn't care. This was just another chapter in what had been a shitshow of a year. She decided then and there that this would be a line in the sand, and next year would be better. She knew she had everything that counted: her children and that fucking heavy ballast box, now half-full of keepsakes, sitting in the back of her car.

And the real heroes had muesli bars.

SJ

Bucket List Buddies

Hans worked hard as a carpenter his whole life and held two lifelong dreams. To explore Germany and his heritage, and to take a cruise. Travel was his great, elusive dream.

Gert worked similarly hard his whole life as a chef in Wandon, in Melbourne's outer north, and always dreamt of an inner-city life; of a nice enough apartment near Melbourne's Yarra River, within walking distance of the Jam Factory cinema complex on Chapel Street in South Yarra. Cinema had always been Gert's great love.

Hans and his family saved for a cruise for Hans soon after his retirement. His ticket was booked and he was looking forward to it immensely. A cancer diagnosis was delivered three weeks before departure. Hans never boarded.

Gert finally realised his dream of inner-city living and acquired a small apartment within walking distance of the Jam Factory. Gert saw not even a handful of films before dying unexpectedly.

Hans ('Opa') and Gert ('Gertie') were Peter B's grandfathers. Two people Peter B loved dearly who just never quite got to do the thing they'd always wanted to do. It taught Peter B how easy it is to not quite get there. How quickly the things you yearn for can be scrubbed from the menu. Peter B resolved to make the rest of his life the best of his life, and to never wait to enact his dreams.

Around this time, at a local footy match in Myrtleford, Peter B's best mate Craig Coombes' voice went all gravelly after a particularly nasty bout of laryngitis. Peter B and Craig Coombes were the ratbag leaders of a tight friendship circle of five fellas. The standard Aussie bloke rule applied: take the piss hard, take the piss always. Craig Coombes' croaky voice provided endless fodder, of course …

'What's that Coombesy, can't quite hear you?'

'Are you trying to barrack again Coombesy?'

'Speak up buddy, I can only hear frog.'

Coupled with the standard array of short, fat and bald jokes, it was quite the fun day.

Craig Coombes' voice never came back fully, though. He loved to sing and never would again, courtesy of a cancer that had wrapped its way all around and down his windpipe. Prognosis? Six to twelve months. Terminal.

There was only one thing for Peter B to do and that was make sure that his best mate, Craig Coombes, didn't die unfinished, like Opa and Gertie, so the first thing Peter B did upon hearing the bad news was ask his best mate the most important question he would ever ask: 'What have you always wanted to do?'

This question yielded a bucket list which Peter B pursued with such relentlessness that the results were commensurately astonishing. He made the impossible possible. The more Peter B reached out, the more came back. Peter B was astounded not just by how accessible people were, but by how genuinely receptive they proved themselves to be. Some of the items on Craig's list disgusted Peter B (like meeting Nickelback, for example), but Peter B dispensed his wherewithal and endeavour free of judgement because 'it wasn't my list, was it!'.

A photo-op with Craig's idol, NRL legend Andrew Johns, turned into coffee and gelato. A chance to meet comedian Adam Hills turned into a starring segment and recurring role on the TV show *Adam Hills Tonight*. A signed CD turned into VIP access and a backstage yarn with Nickelback. A box seat at the footy turned into an on-field tour mid-game and a change-room mingle post-game. A signed photo from actor and singer Christie Whelan turned into front-row seats and the whole cast of *A Funny Thing Happened on the Way to the Forum* – including Christie Whelan, Geoffrey Rush, Hugh Sheridan, Magda Szubanski and Shane Bourne – singing him 'Happy Birthday'. A stranger called Dawn took him for a spin in her red Ferrari, driving him all the way to the Dandenongs for lunch and back. Barry Morgan, from the eponymous stage show *Barry Morgan's World of Organs*, even turned up at Craig's house and pulled out his organ! The list went on and on. Peter B ticked off each item, one by one.

The biggest ticket item on Craig's list was to fly over Antarctica. After an exhaustive call-out and the usual brick walls from corporates, the trip seemed undo-able. The only way for it to happen would be to pay for it, and the money wasn't around. That kind of money never had been. Ten grand.

Peter B and his wife, Deb, mused over it one night together in bed. Deb suggested that Craig's friends and family would all be happy to chip in, but Peter B felt weird about asking for money. Deb wisely told him to get the fuck over it, and a covert army of keyboard warriors was amassed. A secret Facebook group and fundraising page was built. Word spread. Donated goods were secretly raffled and auctioned. Peter B didn't just marry well; turns out he listened well too.

Craig Coombes refers to this stage as 'THE TORMENTING STAGE'. Everybody around him simply shut down on him. He was broadly rebuffed and his loved ones refused to forsake even the tiniest of details. Red herrings abounded. Strategic teasers were thrown out every now and then, just to aggravate him further. Peter B reckons Craig would have pulled out his hair at this stage – if he had any!

Craig's forty-ninth was a film-themed birthday party. Peter B went as a Ghostbuster and Deb went as Scarlett O'Hara. Craig tried to steal the show as a croaky Frank-N-Furter, but costume of the night went to mate Chris, who dressed as a cowboy – not a colourful cowboy mind, no, but as a perfectly shaded cowboy from the black-and-white TV era.

Most of Craig's bucket list items were presented to him that night, either in person, or via video link. All his loved ones flew in from around the globe. Memories were recounted. Laughter emanated. The costumes provided a vivid flair. The drinks and words and gestures ran full and free.

And just when Craig thought it was all over, Peter B silenced the DJ and gathered everyone around.

Peter B asked his best mate if he remembered the biggest thing on his list. Craig Coombes was so bewildered by this point that he couldn't remember a single thing on his list that hadn't been attended to.

So Peter B started reminding Craig about the story from primary school, when little Craig drew the ocean as purple, and through his classmates' laughter and derision had discovered he was colourblind. How Craig made sure the next drawing project at school was white, so there could be no more snickering. How he discovered snow. And Antarctica. How Antarctica and the idea of it had provided him a haven as a boy. How he had always wanted to fly over Antarctica.

The penny dropped. Peter B thanked everyone there who had raised enough for both Craig and his wife, Jayne, to fly over Antarctica, together.

* * *

Opa never went on that cruise. Gertie never saw all those films at the cinema. But thanks to their grandson Peter Buchstaller, Craig and Jayne flew over Antarctica together. According to the pilots on that particular day, the weather was uncharacteristically clear, and they spent an extra hour circling over the most magnificent areas.

* * *

There were two items on Craig's list that Peter B had no control over whatsoever. Craig wanted to become a grandparent, and to walk his daughter down the aisle. Both happened, and Craig was there.

There's nothing left on the list. Now they get the ultimate reward. The time to enjoy the little things. The things that matter most. Peter B still jokes about when Craig 'croaks it', but he's allowed to joke like that, because he's family now.

He's no longer Peter B. Now Craig and his family call him 'Uncle Pete'.

SJ

In for Life

Barbara's twin sister headed off to England and became an international model; she was the glamorous one. Barbara had been telling her mum she wanted to be a nurse for so long that her mum said she'd best get off her backside and get right to it. So she did. It was 1958, when you learnt on the job. She did her four years, then threw on an extra year of learning: obstetrics. But there was more to learn, so Barbara hopped on a boat and went to Vancouver where she caught a train across to Toronto to work in a children's hospital. Amongst the many she cared for were some poor kids from Jamaica, who were often born with malformed hearts. But that wasn't enough for Barbara, there was so much to know. She came home and studied vascular care and when a visiting doctor from Stanford University suggested she go to the United States and work in the cardio transplant unit, off she went. Heart transplants were in their infancy, patients were bleeding out too often, and Barbara wanted to face this conundrum head on. In her spare time, she hit the streets to help feed and support the homeless.

The Vietnam War came along while Barbara was away. Surely she could be of some assistance on the frontline, so she signed up to the US army, even though she was Australian. They did full security checks, though, because clearly the woman was either mad or up to something – why else would she be signing up? Barbara was neither up to something, nor crazy. She just wanted to help. When they figured that out, they sent her for combat nursing training and shipped her off to Vietnam. She and seven other nurses stayed at a rubber plantation on the Cambodian border, abutting a US base. The living conditions were primitive. There was no running water and if they wanted a toilet, they made a hole in the ground. They did have water brought in, though, and the nurses had a makeshift shower. If the doctors wanted to use it, they were quite welcome, as long as the nurses had finished showering first.

One time, a doctor was using their amenities, and some almighty screams cut through the air. When they got there, soldiers in tow, they saw the doctor halfway up the shower pole; there he hung, butt naked, screaming his guts out at a banded krait snake slithering around on the jerry-built floor. After some officers let fly with machine guns, the floor was shot out, no one knew if they'd hit the snake and there stood one very sheepish doctor with no clothes – or pride. Barbara appreciated these lighter moments, in between the thousands of wounded that came through her care. There was just so much blood. Each day a chopper would bring in fresh blood from the Philippines, and the nurses barely had time to check the blood type against a patient's dog tags before pumping it in. They had to make the worst of decisions – they had to decide who was most likely to survive and give those patients their attention.

What does a woman who wants to do the best she can for everyone do next? Well, our Barbara headed to Saigon. There was an artificial kidney unit there, and a whole lot of soldiers with napalm burning their insides out. She and the team tried to neutralise the damage with copper sulphate sticks, but napalm is pretty ruthless and kidney failure was one of the harsh by-products.

After the war, Barbara headed off to Washington State. It was such a beautiful place after being in a war zone, and Barbara assisted with heart transplants. There were lumber camps in the surrounding mountains, and the men who worked there often had coronaries due to the altitude. Barbara volunteered again, feeding and supporting the local homeless when she could. When Barbara caught wind that her mum was sick back home, she returned to take care of her. Her mother recovered, that time, and Barbara headed back out across the globe.

This time she got a job at NASA. The astronauts were all getting osteoporosis and it was time to figure out why. It was difficult to replicate space conditions and really knuckle down to the bottom of that one, but it definitely had something to do with all the radiation in space. Apparently, that's what's holding us up from going to Mars.

After doing what she could there, Barbara joined the flying doctor service. Planes full of doctors, nurses and dentists would go down to the poor villages in Mexico, where health care was scarce but needed. As always, she hit the streets and helped feed and support the homeless in between work.

Barbara's mother got sick again, so she returned to Sydney – her home base. This time her mum didn't make it. Cancer got her siblings over the years too. Barbara doesn't like to talk about her age (she's seventy-eight) and she keeps herself busy by working with the homeless and volunteering with St Vinnies. She doesn't talk about what she does, she simply lists the amazing people doing good work around her. Like Lance, who works out of Martin Place. He has terminal cancer, yet he's still out there delivering food and clothing and sourcing water for farmers. But of course, Lance couldn't do what Lance does without people like Barbara signing up to help. Because it takes a village to effect change, and Lance's village is lucky to have Barbara. A lifetime nurse who kept learning because knowledge saves lives. A lifetime nurse who went to the ends of the earth to use her skills to help out wherever she could. A lifetime nurse who still lends a hand. Because she can.

HH

The Tallest Poppy

Renee was always tall. By fifteen she was six foot five, fully grown and she towered over her peers. For twelve of these fifteen years, little-big Renee had worn a back brace to help her extreme case of scoliosis. The brace was meant to fix her problems without surgery, the experts said. What the experts didn't know was how much little-big Renee got bullied. Kids would run up behind her, smack her on her back brace and call her Big Bird, brace face, or Crusty the Clown (her feet were pretty big). When little-big Renee went to high school, her nickname became 'babs', short for baboon.

At sixteen, Renee finally stood up for herself. She told the experts she wasn't getting any better and that twelve years in that back brace had been for nought. No more waiting for the brace to work; it was time to face the inevitable and have her spine fused and rods put in. The surgery went well, and Renee was able to consider her future. She decided she would focus on taking care of those who couldn't take care of themselves – her path had been determined by those unkind years. Big Renee chose to work in disability care and these days she loves taking her clients out for drives, to the local park, to sit with them at their jobs to help them focus. She enjoys outings with all her clients, but one young man stole her heart. He's half her height and cuddles her a lot. At first he was scared to get off the bus, but not anymore. Now, kicking a ball around the park is both their favourite thing to do together, although it saddens Renee when families pack up their able children and leave when they arrive – she thinks there's still a ways to go in awareness and tolerance.

Renee got cancer a while back, and, as always, took a unique approach to it all. She went to all her chemo sessions in costume. Showtime! For her first treatment, she wore a tiara, and her costume courage grew as her chemo sessions went on. Throughout her first cancer Christmas, she dressed up as a present, Mrs Claus, a stocking and a Christmas tree – with flashing lights, of course. It gave the hospital rooms a lift, and planning her next cancer costume gave her something to focus on. To distract her. One Melbourne Cup day, she dressed as a horse's head – she had to be led to her chemo chair by a nurse as she couldn't see a thing through the enormous head. Renee quickly cottoned on to the value of support and joined the Pink Sisters, and now she co-administers her own support group. They used to have get-togethers at Krispy Kreme, but the group is now fifty strong and the last gathering took up half a Pancake Parlour.

Renee chooses to see the joy in life, and the joy she can bring others. Never mind her renovator's delight body. It is what it is, and she is glad of her experiences back when she was sixteen and had stood up to the experts. When she had cancer and the new set of experts wanted to remove her cancer breast and leave the good one, she again stood tall and told them to take the other ticking time bomb off while they were at it. She's about to have surgery twenty, but she talks about it like it's just another errand to run. Not even a blip on her shine. The support groups have brought her love and friendship, and those isolated school years are a distant memory. If you're lucky enough to stumble across a six-foot-five lady in an Eeyore costume with crocheted nipples, be sure to say hi. It's not just her clients who benefit from her smile and her fun and caring nature – it's everyone she meets.

HH

The Lost Man

Diane loved being a tourism manager with the local government in Western Victoria and revelled in the beauty of the Grampian Ranges. When her job became redundant, she wondered whether police work would suit her. To find out, she thought she would start volunteering with the local State Emergency Service. As she wasn't a great swimmer, she wouldn't be called on for any drowning rescues, but she was as fit as could be. Hiking and running were her strengths, and she settled into the role after her training.

Two Januarys ago, a call came in. There was a missing man in the Grampians. A car was found on some private land at the base of Mount Shelley, and when the police checked the number plates, they connected the car to a man who had been reported missing by his father seven days prior. As most of the local volunteers were on leave and enjoying their summer break, Diane was asked to head over to the site to pitch in. The volunteer manager who had called said they could really use people fit enough to climb the mountain. A local policeman picked her up and they headed off to assist.

On the way, the policeman said that the first day had been a little disorganised, which was common. By day two, there should be shelter, maps, food and drink, and a plan. When they arrived, it wasn't as organised as they'd hoped; they were going to have to fend for themselves to a degree. Of the people present, it was decided that the policeman, Diane and a local farmer were the most capable climbers, so they packed water and fruit into their rucksacks and attached radios to their belts. Off they set, after viewing a photo of the missing man. Diane thought he looked fit and healthy and felt optimistic.

This side of the mountain didn't see much action and there were no walking tracks. Three people didn't constitute much of a line search, but they bush-bashed diligently as they made their way up through the thick scrub. They ignored their growing collection of scratches as they waded through shrubs and pushed tree branches aside. The police helicopter was conducting its own search around them, and it comforted Diane to see them circling. At one point, they discovered some small caves set into the mountain side, and they made sure each one was thoroughly checked. They stayed in radio communication with base as they climbed and battled a cliff face to get to the top. One call suggested that perhaps the missing man may not have survived seven days in the heat and that they should use their sense of smell as well as their eyes. Diane remembered the photo of the missing man and believed he would be found safe. After two and a half hours, they reached the top.

The trio stopped to eat their fruit before continuing. The farmer mentioned a goat track on the western side of the mountain, and Diane wondered if perhaps they should have used it to get up to the top in the first place. Still, it was thorough to cover all sides of the mountain, so she let it go. They did a line search across the top of the mountain. Nothing.

When they reached the goat track on the western side, Diane stopped still. The others followed her lead. 'I can smell him,' she said. The policeman took charge at this point, and said the group should all stop for thirty seconds, and if they agreed that they could all smell him, they would call it in. After ten seconds, he told the others he was going to call the chopper. It had now been four and a half hours since they had set off. Diane, the policeman and the farmer waited where they were while the chopper circled around them, looking for the origin of the smell. They radioed the trio when they spotted him. It turned out he was only twenty metres from where they were standing.

The missing man was behind a tree when they saw him. Diane said he was lying face down like he was asleep with his hands under his face. Diane suddenly sat down. Immobile. Her father had been murdered in a taxi many years before, but it was not until this moment that she thought of the eighteen-year-old girl who had found him. What she must have gone through. She pushed her thoughts away and returned to their mountain-top mission.

When she stood up, the policeman told her and the farmer to wait where they were while he went over to the missing man. He checked the ID in his back pocket and confirmed that he had passed away. It was time for the helicopter to send down an air wing specialist, and a man in a dark blue jumpsuit and a big helmet joined the trio. When he took off the helmet, Diane was chuffed to see a young woman shaking out her blonde hair before introducing herself. She unzipped the massive bag she had brought down with her and explained that it doubled as a stretcher. When she unrolled it, there were two holes and she was relieved when the policeman brought some duct tape out of his rucksack.

They fixed the holes, and Diane was shocked to find out that sealing these holes would stop the body fluids from leaking out of the bag. She reminded herself that she was doing something important. She was helping to get this missing man back to his family.

The air wing specialist was trained to retrieve a body on her own, but the missing man was well over six feet tall, and quite bloated after being in the sun for days, so everyone was given a job. They rationed out gloves, and the two officers rolled the body onto the stretcher, while Diane and the farmer zipped up the bag and helped with the straps. They had to do it in spurts, because the smell and the flies were all too much to do it in one go.

Once the missing man was secured, the trio carried him to a spot nearby, where the helicopter had space to lift him to safety. The air wing specialist attached herself to the stretcher and the policeman held a third rope steady as they were raised into the air. It was windy, and it was important they didn't spin out of control as they were carried away.

When they were gone, the policeman, Diane and the farmer stood in silence. After a while, they contemplated the best way to get back to base. They didn't know where they were anymore, and the goat track was nowhere in sight. As long as they were going down, they figured they'd get to the road eventually. They radioed back to base and asked them to keep honking their horns, so they had a sound to guide them. They were filthy and traumatised, and when they eventually arrived back at base, Diane had no interest in the cheers and back-patting that greeted them. She fought back her tears, ignored the cheers (it did not feel like a success) and headed back to the office with the policeman, where they changed and sent their climbing clothes to be incinerated.

At first, Diane saw a psychologist privately. She didn't want her SES leaders to know, in case they doubted her ability to do her job. She assumed the policeman was used to this sort of thing because he was an experienced officer, so she didn't check in on him. Five months later he took his own life. She doesn't know why, but she knows that what awaited them on top of that mountain that day may have contributed. Along with the car accidents and other scenes he attended as a police officer. It was this that gave Diane a push along. A push along to tell her leaders how much she had suffered. To seek the mental health support available to SES workers. To accept her PTSD diagnosis and to continue her treatment.

The following January, Diane was diagnosed with cancer and she's okay with that. Because it was the cancer that made her mind better. Diane doesn't want to die of cancer, so she embraced the full umbrella of treatment, including meditation and self-care. The things she had resisted in her PTSD battle. Cancer is a disease that comes with research and treatment plans and wellbeing techniques. PTSD is a condition that's less understood, but Diane found if she applied the techniques used to assist her cancer journey to her PTSD, she could help herself. Her prognosis is good. The cancer was caught before making its way to the lymph nodes, so Diane is grateful. Hopeful. She has decided that emergency service work is not for her, but she's excited about her future and what it may bring next.

Every neighbourhood contains SES volunteers and emergency service workers. We thank each and every one of you.

HH

Free 3D Hands

Little Mat grew up in a tight-knit community on Phillip Island. He was a tinkerer, and maintained an unyielding curiosity about how things work and, in turn, how to make things work better. As a kid he would invariably be found in the back shed, disassembling things, repurposing stuff, and blowing things up. He was a maestro with both model aeroplanes and rockets, and found endless satisfaction in his daily search for improvements. Life was fun that way, and his family never impeded him. No helicoptering back then.

One time, little Mat pulled a water pistol apart, removed the motor, bunged a stronger one in and swapped out the

AA batteries for a 9 volt. He duct-taped it all together and presented it to his younger brother, Marc, after he'd tested it. Little Mat's brother shot the modified water pistol into the air and went from feeling like he was squirting a water pistol to feeling like he was shooting some kind of supersonic cannon. Mat will never forget the look of pure joy on his brother's face. *He* had made his brother feel that. By making something work better. In that moment, watching his brother's eyes light up with unadulterated excitement, little Mat realised that he enjoyed making things for other people more than he enjoyed making things for himself. Once he realised that he had the skills to make better stuff for other people, it became an addiction. His path was set. Maybe one day he would make something the whole world could share.

In Year 11 Mat did a year-long exchange to Japan through the Lions Club that would alter his future inexorably. He went from being a middling student who never handed in his assignments on time, to dux of his high school. Mat learnt that in Japan, they do things altogether differently. Through living amongst the Japanese people, Mat learnt the true meaning of unconditional generosity. Respect for others was paramount in their culture. It profoundly changed who Mat was, and how he saw the world. Rather than growing into an individualist, generosity of spirit became his weapon of choice. He committed, after that trip to Japan, to not just making *stuff* better, but to trying to make *the world* better. Somehow. He'd need more than duct tape and dreams though.

Mat's industrious attitude earnt him his desired placement at Monash University, where he elected to study engineering and Japanese. After the first year, Mat got sick of his dad having to hand him fifty bucks to pay for food and decided he would return to Japan, where he could teach English and save enough for the rest of his studies without having to lean on his old man.

After returning home to Australia to complete his degree, Mat did so well at Japanese that he was offered a full scholarship to study engineering at the prestigious Chiba University, back in Japan. As part of his engineering degree in the Chiba prefecture, Mat studied mechatronics, where he was first introduced to a cutting-edge 'bionic arm', which had cost over one million dollars to develop. It was a replacement limb that worked by picking up tiny, naturally generated electric signals in the user's muscles. This was a turning point for Mat. Whoever could afford that type of money? Mat became driven towards a very big dream indeed. A dream of a world where no one who needed a limb would have to pay for it. Not one dollar. A world where every human could move freely.

Before Mat could finish his degree, he was headhunted as a Japanese interpreter at Toyota Australia, which led to the mad scientist job he'd dreamt of. While he studied full time, he worked 105-hour weeks, meaning he was down to a couple of hours sleep a night at best. He'd start at 4 p.m., doing night shifts installing a new press line, be home by 7 a.m., then straight off to uni. This went on for three months while he completed his degree. He was working himself into an early grave. Mat found himself stopping at green lights and going at red lights. He was making bucketloads but had no time to enjoy the spoils. He'd splurge on DVDs at JB Hi-Fi, but they remained in their plastic wrappers. He still has them, wrapped and unseen, as a visible reminder to never burn himself out like that again.

Toyota spent half a million dollars training Mat to improve their processes. To make their business work *better*. Because he spoke Japanese, they sent Mat back to Japan for seven months to learn, bring the knowledge back with him and apply it locally. Mat's job was to make Toyota Australia more sustainable, so they didn't end up offshore.

During these years Mat helped many suppliers become more viable, and they picked up accounts with other auto manufacturers as a result. Mat was now pretty much across the whole manufacturing and engineering thing. In February of 2014, Mat, along with another couple of thousand employees, were mustered into the assembly plant to be told they would all be losing their jobs in three years time.

During the wind-down Mat decided to turn the horridness of the whole situation into something positive. It happened slowly, taking months to materialise. Eventually, Mat accidentally stumbled onto his solution, simply by attending the Avalon Airshow – a popular geek-fest for the technically minded. During Mat's perusing of the pavilions he came across a 3D printer. He observed what was being made and began to think about the possibilities. Current manufacturing techniques didn't allow for most of Mat's blue-sky musings, but there, right before him, stood without doubt a direct bridge to his dream. That world where everyone moved freely.

Mat blew a chunk of his dough on a 3D printer. In the beginning he kept his ambitions realistic. His first goal was to make one hand, for one kid who needed one. Mat started with one finger, controlled by a cheap electronic servo he repurposed from one of his remote-control aeroplanes. During Mat's last years at Toyota he kept his latest finger in his pocket with him while he worked, at all times, to inspire him towards his next step. Mat had access to the world's best design technology right in front of him, so he started going to work an hour early and finishing up late most days, so he could use their software to design better hands (with their permission of course).

Mat encouraged innovation at work by rolling out 3D printers in every manufacturing department, and his ideas were shared at international innovation conferences. He was an investment for the company originally, but now he was the low-cost ideas guy. Many of the ideas that Mat helped generate in those last years at Toyota ended up being adopted globally. Toyota accorded him the title of Karakuri leader (literally meaning 'simple device') and he became one of an elite few cast to find simple solutions to complex problems – his job was to encourage others to innovate in better ways. He got a big kick out of making things simpler and less expensive, which, fortunately, was the very area of expertise he would need to acquire for his blue-sky dream to be achievable.

Mat started collaborating on the internet with people around the world about the latest in 3D printed hand design. He found his people, in all corners, all trying to realise the same dream as his. They shared their ideas freely, in the understanding that they'd get further if they acted collectively. The open-source designs at the time were quite rudimentary and made with basic design software, so Mat was a huge part of the advancements in the field that followed.

After much tinkering, Mat had built the hand to the point where it was able to be used. One in 10 000 kids are born without fingers, but Mat realised that his journey would start with one kid. The first recipient was Little Eli, who lived in Newcastle and needed a hand. Mat asked him to send photos of his arms next to a ruler. He dotted out the measurements. He sent the hand to Little Eli in the post, too busy with his own growing brood to be able to deliver it in person.

A few days later, while he was at his office, Mat received an email with a video attached. It showed Little Eli picking up something for the first time. Then, Little Eli's dad took him to see his mum and show off the new hand at the pub where she worked. They walked in together, father and little son, hand in hand, for the first time ever. Everyone in the pub was in tears. Mat had delivered a single, functioning hand. For one person. For free. He was living his dream.

Mat started making more hands. Many more. As he sent more hands out, he was getting lots of photos from the various families he was assisting. He wanted to see those smiles in real life. There were two girls in Wollongong born without hands. It was only a twelve-hour drive and there was a long weekend looming, so Mat hand-delivered their new hands personally, and saw their smiles for real, for the first time. Word got around. Iconic Melbourne radio host Neil Mitchell caught wind of what Mat was doing, and was impressed by the fact that he didn't just *build* the hand, he drove halfway round the country to deliver it personally. That meant a lot to Neil. Then the mainstream media got a whiff and things began to snowball. Mat's vision started to grow.

Mat became recognised for his volunteer work (his commendations are *ridiculous*). This recognition led to a whole new set of problems for him to solve, as his enterprise grew quickly. He became a poster boy for the retrenched at the same time as becoming publicly recognised for his new work. It was a perfect storm – accolades and awards from the Queen, the PM, etc. Mat thrived surrounded by so many good problems.

Now he has a factory, thirty-odd 3D printers and has founded a charity called Free 3D Hands. Mat hasn't quite got the whole world moving freely yet, but his blue-sky dreams are growing with each hand he provides.

Mat has long been married to his loving and supportive wife Yuka, who he met while studying in Japan as a young man. They've got a couple of kids and his head is still in the blue-sky but his feet are firmly on the ground. Mat plans to walk that ground until everyone has equal access to technology that will improve their quality of life.

Mat is doing what he always has. Finding ways to make things work better. And finding wherever possible the very same excitement from a new kid, with a new hand, that he saw on his brother's face all those years before when Mat supercharged the water pistol in his backyard and learnt he could manufacture joy.

SJ

When the World
Wrote Back

Shannen loves to travel. Each time she came home, from one of the twenty-three countries she has visited so far, she brought a little something back for her best friend – her nan. Even though Shannen FaceTimed her nan from all the places, it was in the lounge room after she got home where they fully relived her experiences: Together. Nan loved wearing the scarf from Scotland, and her replica parrot from Brazil sat proudly on the mantle. Together they dreamt of having a Christmas in New York.

At sixteen, Shannen was offered the chance to experience school life in Rio de Janeiro. Such an exotic opportunity for a girl from country Queensland. Nan and the family sat around the lounge room and organised raffles and garage sales to raise Shannen's airfare. Although she had seen a fair bit of Australia, Shannen had only dreamt of leaving our shores. From the moment she smelt foreign foods and wandered Rio's shanty towns, Shannen knew she wanted to see the whole wide world.

There was only one way to fulfil her future travelling dreams – to be super frugal. While she studied at uni, Shannen had three part-time jobs, ate cheaply, didn't party and scrimped and saved every penny so she could head off again. Europe, Egypt, Morocco, you name it. It wasn't just the places; it was the people. Travelling solo opened opportunities to meet so many, in shoe shops or when grabbing a meal. Each shared moment was treasured. Shannen holds a foreverness from each interaction. But she also loved coming home to Nan. Her confidante, her friend.

When Nan turned seventy-five, she was diagnosed with mesothelioma. Asbestos exposure does that. Sometimes, like in Nan's case, it doesn't surface for years; but when it does, it's nasty. The prognosis wasn't good and Shannen was devastated. All through her childhood, she would walk next door to Nan's house for dinner. They pottered around the kitchen and garden, did each other's makeup, and chatted about life. All through her ups and downs, Nan was her constant; a steady guiding hand while Shannen became. Nan had even homeschooled her for much of her high school years.

Shannen regretted not going to New York for just one Christmas with Nan. Now it was never going to happen. Time was cut short. She wanted Nan to have these experiences of other places, of meeting people from across the globe and swapping stories. To see how other people lived, what they ate, what they sang. So Shannen hatched a plan.

Imagine if she reached out to all the Facebook groups, to all the people she had met, and *they* reached out to all *their* people and so on. Imagine if they all wrote Nan a postcard from all corners of the globe. Then they could travel the world together – without even leaving the lounge room. Shannen knew how easily ideas die, so she set up a post box. She hit the net, told all and sundry about her dear nan who would never have the chance to see the world and she asked everyone she could to send a postcard. She waited a month before checking it. Although there were messages pinging in from all over the place online, it didn't necessarily follow that people would take the time to send Nan a postcard. Shannen knew that loving the idea of something, like a Christmas in New York, doesn't mean it actually happens.

Shannen was so surprised when she checked the post box. There were stacks and stacks of postcards from all over the world. There were letters, and parcels too. Some of them detailed itineraries, some provided old family recipes, some spoke of the imaginary lunch or walk in the park they had with Nan that day. There were pictures of families introducing themselves and their pets from Tahiti to Turkey. There were fridge magnets – a double-decker bus from London, a tea towel from Lisbon with an embroidered crab on it. Nancy from Arizona wrote heaps of cards and letters. No matter where she went, she sent one a day when she was away. Twenty to thirty items turned up a week, from South Africa, India, China, Poland. Even Turkmenistan.

Shannen put all the cards and gifts in a big box, with her own letter to Nan on top. Her letter told Nan that travel isn't about the ticket and going somewhere you haven't been – it's about living all over the world in the hearts of those you meet. She wrote that the people who sent the stacks of cards and letters adored her, just like she did, and that if she couldn't take Nan to the world, she would do her darndest to bring the world to Nan. Well, Nan cried when she realised that so many people were taking the time to write to her, to think of her. So did Shannen. So did the rest of the family. They pored over the contents of the big box for hours on end. Nan really loved the tea towel from Lisbon, not that she played favourites.

Shannen was bang on the money when she said cancer could be cruel and degrading, but boy those postcards created so much joy. Nan was travelling the world without leaving her recliner. And they had the internet to look up the places they knew little about. Nan didn't know much about Turkmenistan, so she and Shannen scrolled through photos and imagined themselves in the Karakum Desert, and atop the Monument of Neutrality.

One of the postcard villagers was an artist from New York. She was so taken by Nan's story that she contacted Shannen to know more. What did Nan love? What were her hobbies? When she found out Nan loved her garden, she asked about the colours and produced a painting. Just for Nan. Knowing how much her granddaughter loved to travel, Nan suggested that Shannen should go and pick it up in person. Never mind her illness. So Shannen arranged a trip and headed over to meet Ashley. The painting was revealed in a cheap motel in West Hollywood, made its way in Shannen's bag to Santa Cruz, then San Francisco and finally home to Brisbane, where it was unfurled. Nan adored this painting; its swirls of blues and greens took her to her garden every time she looked at it. And Shannen had found a new best friend. A friend who crossed the world to be at Shannen's graduation because Nan couldn't make it. Nan had died.

Shannen had always done Nan's makeup before they went out for dinner, or for family occasions, and in true tradition she told the funeral parlour she wanted to prepare Nan's face for her open casket. After some discussion, Shannen went to a cold room and did Nan's makeup. The staff were supportive as she cried over Nan, whose skin wasn't quite the same as before.

But Shannen did a stellar job and Nan looked just as she would have at a family gathering. The family said their goodbyes with the painting and the stacks of postcards sitting proudly up the front.

HH

On the Edge

At sixteen, Nikki's family organised her wedding. It was back in the day when Greek families were all about their daughters getting married and having kids young. Nikki went along with it and had two kids quick sticks, but her family didn't know how violent her husband was until she left him. Nikki did it hard for a few years, largely homeless with the littlies in tow, but she navigated the court system and finally broke free. At twenty-three years of age, with two kids who had seen a lot, she set off for Queensland to start fresh. To settle – so the kids could be from somewhere instead of everywhere.

Nikki never forgot where she came from and started volunteering for various organisations that helped our youth, our homeless. Back in her street days, if she had ten dollars, it would be divvied up with whoever else was down on their luck. Now that she was settling down, she divvied up her time and spent her spare minutes dishing out food and clothes from a sponsored van. In between, she did courses and became a phone counsellor for Lifeline.

Nikki met a new fellow, a drafter by trade, and he supported her pursuits. Fully. When Outreach lost some funding and had to pull Nikki's beloved van, they bought one of their own. So she could continue doing what she loved. Nikki dutifully completed all the required registrations and legal papers and her new charity, On the Edge, was born. They didn't stop at the van either – they purchased a building and converted it into a drop-in centre. By day, Nikki and her crew took the van around to parks for family fun days, where lonely oldies were welcome too, and by night, they hit the local area with vanloads of food, blankets, clothes and hot coffee. Mentor groups for the girls and boys were developed and a lot of those kids, who are in their twenties now, help her out these days.

Nikki has helped multi-generational families who have been victims of trauma. She remembers one house many years ago that looked like a rubbish truck had backed in and dumped its load in the lounge room. Mum would sit on a chair amongst it all, surrounded by pills and empty baked bean cans full of ciggie butts. Her daughter went to a local school and Nikki helped her out with shoes and food. Before long, Nikki began spending time with the whole family. When you go around the classroom and ask kids what they want to be when they grow up, no one says a gambling addict, a drug user, homeless. Nikki knows very well that addiction occurs because of other issues; that it's a coping mechanism. People end up where they end up and providing other pathways can create change.

That mother no longer sits in the filth with her remote control as her only friend. She embraced Nikki's guiding hand, cleaned up her house and her life and she's now a doting grandma who helps Nikki out when she can. It's not always a happy ending, though. A young man Nikki helped get clean, get housing and even get his daughter back took his own life. This tragedy inspired Nikki to add a new goal to her growing collection. A 24-hour house is next on her list, and no doubt she'll find a way.

A while back, Nikki's husband's business began to shrink. Corporations were sending their drafting projects overseas. Why pay fifty bucks an hour here when you can send the project elsewhere for five bucks an hour. It meant that Nikki had to scale back some of her projects and rethink her charity. There was never any talk of selling the building or the van, it was a matter of finding other ways to fund her dreams. The front part of the drop-in centre became a cafe. That way they could still feed the homeless and get the community to fund it. The locals came in droves, and their reputation for having the best eggs benny going around spread. It wasn't the only thing that spread. Word of her exploits did too.

Nikki's a bum up–head down kind of lady, and she didn't realise that if you educate the community, they'll hop on board too. Nikki's sidekick, Frances, is the mouthpiece, the one telling all the locals about their mission and garnering support. The voice over your shoulder while you chow down on your eggs benny. Nikki's still bum up–head down in the back of the cafe, welcoming anyone who needs a shower, some fresh clothes or counselling. The kids who had seen a lot now have kids of their own, and they pitch in to help Nikki show people that there are other paths. Paths they walked themselves, all those years ago.

HH

Behind the Badge

The policeman:

Radio call, set of 83s – report of death for the coroner. Deceased two-month-old female found by parents in a cot.

The man behind the uniform:

There's a chill in the air and he can see wispy breath clouds swirling around his face. The cold air creates pins and needles in his lungs as he walks towards the house. It almost distracts him from what lies ahead. Keep breathing those needles. He glances at his partner and wonders if she feels the same.

The policeman:

Meet the ambos at the door. Handover. Two-month-old child confirmed deceased. Body cold, so death a few hours prior. Mother hadn't heard from the child, went to check, called ambos – too late. Enter with partner.

The man behind the uniform:

It's dimly lit and warm inside. The young mother is sitting on the couch holding her little girl swaddled in blankets. The image oozes love. Other than her eyes being red, there is no sign of anything out of place. The room is full of baby things and the stuffed big bird toy is smiling. Such a cosy room.

The policeman:

Has a crime been committed? Parents do kill their children. Facts for the coroner. Radio call. Detectives on their way. Make assessment, establish crime scene if required.

The man behind the uniform:

The radio calls and he's relieved to leave the room. Is he a coward for leaving his partner to talk to the mum? He tells himself she's more experienced, but that doesn't make it any easier for her. His heart swells as he enters the nursery. It's warm and lit so softly. It's clean and tidy and packed full of baby things. It's what a nursery should be. There's a strewn aside blanket in the cot, as there would be every time a mother reaches to clasp her crying baby. The death bed. His throat feels like he's swallowed a golf ball. He returns to the living room and both parents are talking to his partner, choking on tears and grief. All eyes have degrees of tears. He blinks his away and saves them for later.

The policeman:

Detectives arrive. Go to front step and detail the scene. Detectives enter. Explain their presence. When there are no reasons for a child's death, it must be investigated. Tour the nursery. The body to be checked for signs of visible trauma.

The man behind the uniform:

He delicately helps the detectives unwrap the tiny, cold body. Her distraught mum wants to help. Their non-medical minds see there's nothing wrong. This poor woman. But he can't rush to judgement, the autopsy might show ... this poor mother ... they need an undertaker to ... oh this tiny, tiny body.

The policeman:

Foul play not ruled out, but unlikely. Deceased baby to go to the Victorian Institute of Forensic Medicine. Back to the station for paperwork.

The man behind the uniform:

There's a glimpse of breaking dawn as the ambulance drives away. He takes a deep breath and the smallest of moments to reflect in the crisp stillness. This big breath of cold air cleans out the smell of death, well, perhaps physically. They don't talk much on the way back to the station. They're dealing with the scene in their own ways. Separately, yet together.

HH

Walk and Talk

What do you want? What do you want to do with your life?

These are confronting, complex questions; questions that many adults prevaricate over for much of their life, let alone the swathes of teenagers graduating from high school each year – mostly too inexperienced or ill-equipped to yet fully comprehend their own true yearnings and ambitions.

Jodie Wood proved no exception as she came to the end of her secondary education in East Gippsland. If Jodie knew one thing, she knew she wanted to do something of benefit to others. She wanted to help people. At seventeen, she and her parents agreed that teaching seemed a good fit and was likely her best path, so Jodie enrolled for a Dip. Ed., but not before a gap year. To get by she hustled in hospitality with split shifts and shitty pay. Through her work in hospitality she encountered her fair share of lost souls who spent their lives staring into the bottom of their beer glasses, broken and bummed out. She saw firsthand, and for the first time really, just how vulnerable people could become. Her heart started bleeding for the people without enough to lean on.

She studied teaching for a year before seriously questioning her decision. Did she really want to work with children? Strangely, it was the adults who seemed most in need. So Jodie decided the oldies needed her more than the kidlets and re-enrolled to study aged care. She had found what she wanted to do. Not before another gap year, though!

Jodie is forty-five and back in her home town of Clifton Creek now, living with her partner, James, and working with the oldies at the local aged-care facility. She lives a stone's throw from the house she grew up in. She's been through cervical cancer, which has scuppered her ambitions to be a mother, so she directs her love to James and her big Alaskan Malamute 'fur baby' rescue dog, Ella, who's been by Jodie's side since she was a six-week-old pup.

Clifton Creek is a small underdog town, off the main highway, largely ignored by the shire in favour of larger surrounding towns along the highway. Population 260, give or take. It's hard to make a living in Clifton Creek, and many of its townsfolk experience genuine hardship. Chronic drought for the past eight years has driven the despair.

Through these harsh years, Jodie found herself so exhausted by her work hours and so busy with her own family that she tended to exist in her own bubble. She had minimal contact with the community, but when she did come across the odd local needing a chat, she'd walk with them. Being a bit of a rescuer, Jodie was always more than happy to listen, and those keen for an ear seemed to gravitate towards her. Jodie developed an ethos, a mantra – 'Walk and Talk'. She'd get people out. To walk and talk. And it worked. Slowly, Jodie became more involved in her community.

Soon everyone would know her name.

The day the 'forever fires' hit Clifton Creek it was well over forty degrees, over forty-five in some parts. The conditions were horrific and the weather bureau showed no change in sight. Jodie had decided to stay and defend. She lived on a small hobby farm and her animals meant everything to her. If she didn't protect the hayshed and the animals survived the fire, they would starve, and Jodie wasn't having a bar of that.

Back just a few years there were fires on the bush line at the edge of their town. But miraculously the wind changed just in time and took the vicious firewall in another direction, and the town was saved. Jodie, along with the rest of the town, knew that this time Clifton Creek wouldn't be so lucky. They sat in the middle of the fire's path. It had been coming for weeks.

Disasters can bring out the best in some people. Jodie became very active and started liaising with locals weeks before the fires hit. Walk and talk. She encouraged others to either leave, or stay and defend; and to make their decision early. She reminded everyone not to expect a fire truck at their house when the shit hit the fan. To not expect any help at all. The fire was too big for the emergency services to protect everyone. She helped some leave, she helped others prep, all the while taking measures around her own property. Everyone who stayed in Clifton Creek dug in and helped one another.

Jodie's hobby farm sits basically in the middle of the township on a little rise, giving her a direct view over the town to the surrounding bush. The fire came quick and it came hard, over the bush line, into the open country and onto private properties. There was chalky ash everywhere, horrific heat, embers. Explosions could be heard from houses up the road, then the school ignited. The smells will never be forgotten. The smell of bush burning, plus all the plastics and goodness knows what else. It sounded and smelt and felt like the end of days.

Adrenaline kicked in. By the time Jodie and James had activated their sprinklers and fire pumps, their back bush had already been engulfed. Jodie sent James to the hayshed to start the pump and hosed the house as spot fires raged around them. Visibility was down to five metres tops. Their adrenaline was pumping so hard they both forgot to use their radios. They stood only metres apart, with a hose each, wetting the house and hayshed, but they couldn't see each other at all. So they yelled.

'I'M OKAY!'

Then they'd wait for the other …

'I'M OKAY!'

Sometimes there would be no reply but they both knew if they let go of their hoses they'd lose their bearings. So they'd scream again and wait.

Back and forth it went, through the squall, hour after hour. Jodie and James fought the fire until 4.30 the following morning, when Jodie finally deemed it safe enough to send James inside for a nap. Unless anything changed, they would now take turns, one keeping watch as the other rested. It went like that, taking shifts to put out spot fires, for the next three days.

Somehow, the animals were saved. And the machinery. The house also. And, most importantly to Jodie, the hayshed still stood, meaning her small, precious brood of cattle and sheep would not go hungry during the recovery. Her fur baby Ella was safe and sound. Everything important was saved.

The town was heavily affected, though. The school and six houses were gone. That's a lot for a town that small to contend with. Luckily, all the unaccounted for were found. Lots of injuries, property and stock losses, but thankfully no human casualties in the end.

After the fire, Jodie clicked into gear. She drove to a neighbouring town and asked a local food bank for help. They were more than happy to oblige, and filled Jodie's station wagon with food and water. Jodie then went door to door in Clifton Creek doing welfare checks and offering care packages. Power was out and household food was ruined. It was dangerous stuff. Burning trees and spot fires impeded her progress. Just reaching some of the properties was hairy.

As she visited people, Jodie was impacted heavily by their reactions. Some were emotional, some were dumbstruck and silent, all were traumatised. Jodie reminded them that they weren't alone, that aid was coming, to hang tight.

Jodie put the call out on social media for help, and volunteers rushed to the town. Given she'd put the call out, Jodie was thrown the set of keys to the community hall, which was still intact, and before she knew it she was wrangling dozens of volunteers, hiring portable showers and spearheading the recovery effort.

Jodie knew of the divides that existed between the people in her community. She instituted a town barbeque every night during the aftermath and, being the rescuer that she is, she decided to invite the people she knew didn't get along. She deliberately put together people who hadn't spoken for years. Sure enough, the town was bonded by the experience and many old bridges were mended during those barbies.

The town's new Community Recovery Committee (CRC) is chaired by Jodie, and she has invited one member from each community group to join her on it. She cold-called Ken Lay, the former police commissioner who was soon to be head of Bushfire Recovery Victoria, and convinced him to visit Clifton Creek. This brought much-needed attention to the town and its needs. Jodie's role now is to make sure every single member of her little community is tended to, cared for and supported through their own rebuilds.

She's found a friend to help her too: a musterer, a fencing contractor and a cracking bush poet by the name of Ken Stuart. They fix fences together and every day he'll belt out a poem or two. She loves him and reckons his poetry is top notch. Together they're about to hold a combined birthday party/working bee, because there's still so much to do.

Jodie's property remains as it was when the fires hit. Sure, she, hubby James and the bush poet will get around to repairing her property – but not before everyone else's is finished.

Clifton Creek is an underdog town with a champion now. Her name is Jodie and these days everyone in town knows her name. She's the one who's always good for a walk and talk. She's the one with the bush poet sidekick. She's the one person every town needs. A hero next door.

SJ

Hearts the Size
of China

Guy promised his big sister that he would bring up her kids if she died. Michelle was pregnant with her second child when she was diagnosed with breast cancer. She chose to see out the pregnancy and worry about treatment later. Her baby daughter was born healthy and Michelle underwent a range of treatments, but the cancer had spread. Michelle died. Guy says their mother took it the worst. Although she had gained a granddaughter, she had lost a daughter, who may have survived if the pregnancy had been terminated. Guy acknowledged that this may be true, but he respected Michelle's choice and began a year-long legal battle to get custody of Michelle's two daughters, aged seven and two. Guy was twenty-two years old.

A few months before Michelle died, Guy got married. Michelle was a proud bridesmaid, and although she was in a wheelchair, somehow, she stood for the ceremony. Guy's voice still cracks as he speaks of her sheer determination. Even after all these years. The siblings danced together at the reception. It was the last time Michelle stood up.

Guy worked in a car factory in South Australia and his wife worked in radiology. They worked hard during those earlier years and it was tough financially. Having lost his sister, he was grateful each day to wake up with his bum pointing to the ground and to have a job to fund his life. He would say this to anyone at work who would listen. The lawyer who helped them gain custody of their instant family told them to pay off their fees when they could and, despite the debt, they secured a humble first home. Sometimes they had to count out five-cent pieces to buy bread and milk. The family got up each morning and had breakfast together before Guy's wife went to work and he took the kids to day care and school. He'd get some shut-eye, do a brief handover when his wife got home, and then head off for night shift. They planned to have a bunch of kids themselves, but wanted to pay off more of their house before they tried for a baby. This was their life for a few years. At the grand old age of twenty-six and twenty-seven, they decided that they were ready to have children of their own.

They had another daughter and Guy was proud as punch. Just when they were juggling life with a newborn, Guy took himself off to the doctor. He knew something was wrong and he was sent for scans. This was back in the days before emails, and he was given a letter to take to his GP – as soon as possible. Guy opened the letter, but it may as well have been written in Mandarin. He stopped for petrol on his way home and rang his wife on his fliptop Nokia. He had moved from the factory floor to warehousing and was running a small team these days. He and his wife worked hard and both took pride in their new phones. He told her he had been for scans and read out the words he didn't understand. She began sobbing on the phone before he even got halfway through the letter. He knew it was bad news but didn't push her for answers. Instead, he went to the doctor – testicular cancer.

Guy was a thorough young man. He had to be to run an instant family at so young an age. He did some research and found that treatments for testicular cancer, unlike his sister's breast cancer, were simple and effective. They had found it early and treatment had a roughly 80 per cent success rate.

For four months, the family struggled in many ways. The treatment left Guy so tired, so incapacitated, that he couldn't work to support his family or help his wife with the girls. Guy says his wife is the true hero in this tale. He says she didn't think twice about taking on his nieces back when they were newlyweds, she just dove in. It was a package deal, and she stood up. So, Guy's wife stood up again, took some leave and ran the household for four months while he underwent treatment and recuperated between chemo sessions. Back to counting out five-cent pieces for milk and bread.

Guy was one of the lucky ones. He was given the all-clear. The bitter pill was that they wouldn't be able to have more children. This was difficult because they desperately wanted to expand their clan. Before beginning chemo, Guy had frozen some of his sperm, so they went through five cycles of IVF. None took. Husband and wife sat down at the dinner table after the kids had gone to bed one night and decided, together, to accept their fate.

Guy went back to work and received another promotion, and his wife was back at work too. They were grateful for their three girls and decided to plan their dream home. They worked, they planned, they built, all the while enjoying their girls and embracing family life. They had great work–life balance and slowly their dream home took shape.

On the big night of their housewarming party, Guy was heading out the door to buy the wine. His wife said she felt a little funny, and perhaps he should pick up a pregnancy test while he was out. He scoffed at the impossible, got the wine and picked up a pregnancy test anyway – nothing wrong with dreaming from time to time. Home he went, to the loo she went. It was positive. Guy enjoyed the wine at his party (his wife didn't), and it took all his strength to keep the secret from his friends and family all gathered there together. The couple went to the doctor the following week and the pregnancy was confirmed. The doctor shook his head and said they had more chance of winning the lotto than getting pregnant. They had a son.

Car manufacturing had come to a standstill by the time their son was born, but Guy applied for and got the position of general manager of spare parts. He felt so blessed. It gave him the chance to remind a whole new team that they should be pleased as punch every day that they woke up. That their bums pointed to the ground. That they had a job, family, kids.

Not too long after that, Guy's wife felt funny again. Off he went to get a pregnancy test, and again they had won the lotto. Another son. Guy and his wife sat down after dinner one night and discussed something they thought would never be on their agenda after his battle with testicular cancer – contraception. There were no more children, but the house was full and happy. The company closed down, and within days, Guy was offered a position in Melbourne.

As they often did, Guy and his wife sat down at the dinner table and discussed their options. His sister's daughters were grown and had moved out. Maybe it was time to take a punt and move interstate. They agreed to take a chance and just do it.

Their youngest children are now in their teens and Guy has settled into his new job. His youngest niece has followed the only parents she has ever known and moved to Melbourne with her daughter, and his mother will be moving over in the new year. The magnet, the glue, the gel of Guy and his wife is such that the rest of the family are moving over to be together again. Guy has five grandchildren to enjoy and still tells everyone who works in the factory that each day they are lucky to wake up. To have a job, so they can enjoy their family, their lives. To have their bums point to the ground.

HH

Blind Luck

Big Dave was a big kid, had cataracts and great big bulletproof glasses, half a golf ball thick. Other kids learnt quickly not to tease him for it. Whenever Big Dave ended up in a punch-on, the teachers always took his side. They'd tell him that he couldn't keep hitting people, then more seriously reprimand the antagonists for instigating. The teachers knew Big Dave to be sensible and well spoken, like his dad, and he only struck out when provoked, so their lenience with him was earnt.

Big Dave and his brother, Peter, had a great dad. He was even tempered and always respectful. Unlike some of the other fathers around at that time, Big Dave's dad never raised a hand in anger towards his kids, although they didn't see an awful lot of him, because he was a hard-working fella – an industrial electrician.

Horses delivered milk in carts back then. Big Dave and his less adventurous older brother, Peter, got up to plenty of mischief, just like any other young brothers might, and their childhood was spent riding their bikes or walking through the apple orchards, often with Big Dave's best friend, Chris. Always through the orchards. They floated through their youths, through the orchards, without any major dramas 'more through good luck than good management', Big Dave reckons. Big Dave wasn't half as lucky as his father, though.

Christmas Eve, 1978. It was a hot day. Big Dave, ten, sat excitedly on the bench-seat of their dad's cream-coloured panel van. They were off to 'take a squizzie' at some mudbrick homes in Eltham. Being so close to Christmas, Big Dave remembers being in an excitable mood – ten is a good age for Christmas. On the way, Big Dave's dad had to stop by a mate's place to do a quick job. This was a home job, more a favour than anything else, and shouldn't take too long.

Big Dave watched his dad work, blue overalls on as always, pulling out a cable from inside a wall cavity to connect onto the switchboard. He watched his dad slip as he pulled at the stubborn cable and stab himself just under the eye with his long-nose pliers. The pliers went in deep. Real deep. But Big Dave's dad had a high pain tolerance and wasn't prone to carry on; he just cursed, grabbed some electrical tape and plugged his wound with it. He told his kids not to worry, and that he'd finish the job then get to the hospital. The mudbrick joint in Eltham would have to wait for another day.

Big Dave remembers Christmas that year very well. They never called it cancer. The doctors found a big melanoma behind Big Dave's dad's eye. Stabbing himself with the long-nose pliers was the best thing that could have happened to him. He wasn't just lucky to be alive; stabbing himself saved his life, literally. If he hadn't, the melanoma would've progressed unchecked and he wouldn't have stood a chance. Blind luck.

The doctor wanted to take the melanoma and the eye out, but Big Dave's dad wanted a second opinion. When Big Dave was just a little boy, his cataracts had been falsely diagnosed and Big Dave's dad had been sceptical of doctors ever since. So he went home to be with his family for Christmas, eye intact, and contemplated his next move. Supporting his family depended on his depth of perception, and he didn't want to lose the eye unless absolutely necessary.

Big Dave's dad found a new doctor after Christmas. This new doctor was way ahead of his time and suggested sealing the melanoma with a laser and keeping the eye. It was highly unorthodox, but Big Dave's dad went right ahead, had the melanoma lasered, and held onto his sight. Whatever that doctor did worked. For forty years.

Big Dave grew up and ended up working in England as a young man. At twenty-six, he noticed an irregularity downstairs. He knew. He just knew. After the diagnosis came through, he rang his family back in Australia to let them know he had testicular cancer. His dad thought he was joking at first. His family took it hard, but Big Dave got on with it and leant into treatment and all that goes with it. He didn't want an implant. In Big Dave's words, 'It's a good cancer to get. One less testicle. Still here. Three kids.'

Big Dave's brother ended up getting cancer as well. Peter was also 'lucky'. Bowel cancer forgives very few, but Peter has been twenty years clear.

Big Dave's mum was next. At seventy-nine, she was diagnosed with breast cancer. According to Big Dave, 'Mastectomies are difficult, no matter how old you are. She's tough as nails, though, and four years cancer free.'

Big Dave's best mate followed. Chris. The doctors struggled with this cancer. It was a particularly rare kind that took time to diagnose, and we know how that goes. The staff at the hospice liked Big Dave and his terminal mate, Chris. They helped him out to the park one night for his last breath of fresh air. Big Dave had Scotch and crayfish with his best mate that night. They knew it was their last night together.

So we come to today. Everyone in Big Dave's family has had cancer, including him, and they've all survived. So far.

Big Dave is trying to be as good a dad as his own father was, to his three children, and life is moving on. But Big Dave wonders sometimes. He wonders about those orchards from when he was a kid.

They all walked through those orchards. All the time. And who knows what we put on our crops back then, right?

SJ

Good Different

Jimmy considered himself a lucky kid, in that he doesn't remember ever being alone. As the second eldest of seven, along with the swag of friends that accompanied his parents' open-door policy, there was always someone for Jimmy to be with. He liked being included in his sister's doll's house role-plays, but he sat just outside of the performances. He kicked the footy with his brothers, but he was clearly hopeless at sports, so he sat just outside of his brothers' pastimes too.

Never being alone is not quite like *feeling* alone, or apart, and there was a phantom feeling growing in Jimmy's tummy. An unease of sorts, a sense that he didn't quite belong, at least not in the same way his siblings seemed to belong to each other. The more he tried to comprehend the source of his unease, the more crippling his confusion became. Nothing apparent was wrong, so why didn't he *feel* right? It was a totally private issue. A sore tummy was permissible to discuss, but not a twisted, knotty one that wouldn't go away. It was his private phantom menace. His secret secret.

Life went proper south for young Jimmy when high school hit. He wasn't the same enough, was promptly shoved in the 'not worth a pinch of shit' basket, perhaps partly because of his small size and natural benevolence. Regardless, this unsurprisingly intensified Jimmy's existing confusion.

Perhaps because of the sturdiness of his large, tight-knit family, Jimmy thankfully didn't believe what was said about him – no matter how much it hurt. He *knew* they were wrong. He was good different and he would prove it to every moronic detractor. Jimmy's pain built itself into a very strong determination to demonstrate that he wasn't what they said he was. He didn't know how yet, but he knew he would show them.

At fifteen Jimmy did work experience at the local, community-minded Croft Cafe, where he acquitted himself skilfully enough to score a full-time gig, after school every day and Saturdays too. It was a family cafe, with local art for sale on the walls, and Jimmy found that there he wasn't told to be anyone else. Jimmy built solid bonds with the regulars and it made him feel good. Feeling wanted built a sense of belonging and his tummy stopped twisting so much. And he got paid!

Linda and Geoff were Jimmy's favourite customers. They shared Jimmy's natural benevolence and got on terrifically with him. Linda and Geoff's daughter Jayne had a daughter called Emily, who came in occasionally, always sporting a beanie and always in a wheelchair, with tubes coming out of her nose. Jimmy had never seen someone with cancer before in his life, let alone a child, and was taken aback by her habit of smiling at everyone and always trying to make others feel comfortable. It put pangs in his heart. Here was this sick girl, more worried about her chair being in the way of others than by the tubes in her face. Emily was good different too. They got along famously, and Jimmy's kinship with the family grew.

One random day Jimmy's phone rang. It was his boss, letting him know that little Emily wouldn't be coming into the cafe anymore. She had died overnight. Jimmy hung up and felt an instant rage burn up through his insides. He had never experienced anything so intensely before. Jimmy bolted home, opened his laptop and through sweaty, furious tears, typed 'how the fuck do I cure cancer' into his search engine. Something had to be done for that poor, innocent girl. Emily had been diagnosed with leukemia at three years of age, beat it by five, got brain cancer at six and was dead by eight. *How could this happen?*

On the internet, Jimmy learnt of a woman called Deb De Williams, who had walked around Australia *twice*. She did her first lap to raise money for Helpline after losing a loved one to suicide, then, after beating a cancer diagnosis, she did *another* lap of the country for cancer research. She was actually on her third lap during Jimmy's research phase!

Young Jimmy decided then and there, on the same day he received the news of Emily's passing, that if Deb De Williams could do something so epic, then so could he. Jimmy wasn't athletic *at all*, but he could walk. And he was angry enough to walk further than too far.

Jimmy graduated from high school during his planning phase, which took fifteen months. General consensus from his schoolmates was 'tell him he's dreaming', and many of the sponsors he approached for support told him he was too young, and to try something smaller first. Their collective lack of faith only served to strengthen Jimmy's resolve, although he of course went through the necessary periods of self-doubt that accompany any significant undertaking. His mental health was shot. The only way to truly deal with the fear and self-doubt was to start walking.

Jimmy walked twenty-two million steps in homage to an eight-year-old girl he technically didn't even know that well. It took over one year to complete. Along the way he raised truckloads of cash for the Brainchild Foundation. Jimmy turned Emily's tragic death into a glorious, year-long celebration of her life. He shared Emily's story everywhere he went.

Jimmy didn't 'find himself' at the end of his 'journey'. And while he had started out wanting to prove his detractors wrong, that didn't truly motivate him for long. You need more than that to go further than too far. Jimmy was, however, proving something to himself. Not necessarily proving himself *as* anything, rather proving to himself who he *wasn't*. He demonstrated to himself, in the most extreme way possible, that he was worth way more than a pinch of shit. That he wasn't worthless. Or weak. Or a guy with no chance in life.

Now Jimmy is back home, that thing in his tummy that plagued him throughout his youth has gone. He no longer feels like he's sitting outside of his loved ones. When the opportunity presented itself, Jimmy told his family he was gay. There wasn't even a ripple, let alone the disapproval he feared. Not even close; it was, quite literally, not a thing at all. If anything, his family love him more now because they know him better. Plus they're super proud of that epic walk he did.

Jimmy is crazy stupid in love with a kind-hearted guy who loves him for who he is, who sees him as good different. Because Jimmy knows who he *isn't*, and that's a pretty attractive quality for a kid in his mid-twenties.

Jimmy's going to uni now, and he's going to become a school counsellor, to help the other little Jimmys out there in other high schools, who get told they aren't worth a pinch of shit.

SJ

All at Sea

When Christine joined the navy, women couldn't be pilots or mariners. They held land jobs – to free the men up to go overseas. Christine's passion was the cadets. Kids between thirteen and eighteen joined up, and although they were not part of the defence force, they were part of the defence force family. They got issued uniforms, which are the same as those in the military, and they participated in activities that included power boating, abseiling, sailing and weapons training. After security clearance, the cadets could go and stay on board naval ships. It wasn't just about the activities. It was about building confidence in our young. Promoting honesty, integrity, a team culture. Giving them leadership skills, empowering them to become community-minded citizens.

In the mid-eighties, the Women's Royal Australian Naval Service (WRANs) was dissolved. No more service within a service. They were amalgamated into the navy and it was acknowledged that women could do the same jobs as men. But the transition to acceptance was not immediate.

Christine remembers an off-the-cuff question by a male counterpart: 'How's the petticoat command going?' Christine muttered a 'fine thanks' and went about her job as commanding female officer – a position that was originally given to a man. When he had been deployed overseas, Christine had stepped into the role and took charge of her cadets; females welcome. She explained to the powers that be that she was doing the job anyway, and pointed out that her predecessor didn't look like he was coming home anytime soon, and so she ended up in the role she was overlooked for in the first place.

When girls were first allowed into the cadets, their numbers were capped at twenty; extras were placed on a waiting list before the joining process equalised. Christine found that the girls were committed and took great pride when they were able to skipper a sailing boat, obtain power boat licences and perform in the ceremonial guard. After a while, they were given the same uniform as the boys (no more skirts), they were allowed to carry weapons and they took part in Anzac Day and Remembrance Day ceremonies.

At the beginning of change, male cadets saw the cadets as a service for boys. They were following the prejudices of the day and didn't know otherwise. On one occasion, some of the boys refused to attend training because the squad leader was a girl. Christine wasn't judgemental. She explained that it was their choice to boycott activities and held firm. Eventually they would realise they were only fighting themselves and return. Which they did.

In the 1990s, Christine stood proudly in front of an all-female catafalque guard. It's not easy being on reverse arms for a length of time, and it's not uncommon to see members fainting. There were lots of people watching, and it's still a common memory that is talked about today.

Christine never forgot the 'petticoat command' comment, and she worked hard to prove that female cadets were as valuable and committed as the males. She has loads of awards, showing her cadets were rated the most efficient cadet unit not just in Queensland, but in Australia. Over her 28-year career, she helped over seventy cadets enter the Royal Australian Navy. Twenty-five per cent of those cadets were females. Females she encouraged through a time when girls weren't seen as being capable of doing the job. Through times when she wasn't considered capable of doing the job. She stood firm and her thanks was watching her female cadets not just join the navy, but climb the ranks.

HH

Ken was ranked sixteenth out of nineteen children, and went on to have eight himself. As a young man, he caught the bus to work and one day, a plucky young lady who had been eyeing him off for a while mustered the courage to ask him to the local dance. He accepted the invitation and they never left each other's sides thereafter. Ken and Lorraine married on New Year's Day in 1955, and the children came quickly. One marriage wasn't enough for these two lovebirds – they renewed their vows on their twenty-fifth and fiftieth anniversaries as well. In the same little church in Clayton where they first tied the knot all those years before. Back when the outer Melbourne suburb of Clayton was brimming with market gardens, horses and carts and the odd foundry. Husband and wife stayed with the in-laws for a couple of years while the young couple found their feet.

When kids three and four came along, twins, Ken and Lorraine packed up and moved to Ferntree Gully. It was close to a variety of cousins and they had a pine forest at the end of their street. Ken had a job as a can man. Before sewerage infrastructure, chaps used to come around in a truck, remove the can from under people's backyard toilets and carry the cans to their truck to empty them. These cans were transported on the shoulders, and often on the heads, of can men, and occasionally the bottom fell out of them. Number 2 of Ken's 8 recalls the time Dad came home and yelled through the house for mum to 'bring the hose and the phenyl'. To get rid of the sewage dripping off him. Lorraine was grateful this career didn't last too long, and Ken happily went off to a new job in a rubber ball factory. 2 of 8 remembers these years fondly. Playing amongst the trees, making mud pies and hanging around with all the cousins and neighbourhood kids. More siblings came along, so they never wanted for company.

Ken got a break and secured a good job on a railway gang. It did mean uprooting the family, and off to Kilmore East they went. The railways always moved families at

Christmas time, so they were a little late to save the local primary school. The school had been a few kids short of being viable, so when Ken and his brood turned up, the kids had to bus it into Kilmore proper.

It was a golden time for the kids. When they waited for their school bus home, they walked over the road to see the pigs. There was a part factory, part abattoir over the road, and they were always given some warm, smoky bacon from the curing racks. They played in the mud around the pub and the post office until Ken got promoted to head gang on the railways, and off the troupe went again.

When the family arrived at their allotted railway house in Donnybrook, Lorraine shook her head and walked across the street to the local phone box. She rang the Railway Institute and asked them exactly how they were expected to live in a two-bedroom home with eight kids. The very next day, a bunch of fellows turned up and began building their bungalow. The two boys went into the smaller side, the four biggest girls got the bigger side and the younger two had the second bedroom in the house. Sorted. They were a team, and Lorraine had this one. Just as Ken had the night shift with the babies. If a child cried in the night, it was Ken who got up to feed them, change them, comfort them. It was Lorraine's turn to rest. He was a sensitive new age guy before SNAGs were even invented.

All eight kids grew up with a hands-on dad. With team-based parents. They always backed each other up. There was no 'yes' from one and 'no' from the other. They were united. And the kids thought it was gross how they kissed each other. Their displays of affection were there for all to see; visible love. If Mum wasn't home, Dad would pace around. He was only truly comfortable when his bride, his love, was right there with him. The whole family was a unit. If Mum and Dad were invited to a wedding, they would only go if all the kids were invited too. They were not an unruly group. They had manners, they were respectful, and they did everything together.

As they got older, it became even more evident how much Ken and Lorraine cared for each other, doted on each other, doted on their family. Railway work had become a younger man's game, so Ken and Lorraine worked in pubs for the following years. Together. Ken front of house, Lorraine managing the kitchen. When the grandkids came to stay, any sign of a stirring in the night would see Ken up and about to sort it out, telling their mothers to go on back to bed for some shut-eye.

After a long working life, Ken and Lorraine moved to Yea, a country town north-east of Melbourne. To retire. They loved Yea, and Yea loved them. Yea's the sort of town where you're only a local if you were born there, but that didn't stop Ken and Lorraine becoming locals. Ken immediately joined the RSL. Although he hadn't served overseas, he'd done his nasho – two years national service. He and Lorraine helped set up the Yea Neighbourhood Watch, and they were embraced. All their time was spent bettering the community. Liaising with the local MP, the local police, the schools and the scouts. They were in their element. Of an evening, Ken and Lorraine sat together – they never missed the nightly ABC news.

As they entered their twilight years, Lorraine had a turn and had to go to Melbourne and stay in hospital for a few days. Although it all turned out okay, Ken worked himself up into a lather. He had a panic attack while he paced the floor waiting for her, and he thought it was a heart attack. He went off to hospital too. It didn't work out as well for Ken, he was sick. He was diagnosed with lung cancer, and off he and Lorraine went to Melbourne for eight weeks of treatment.

Ken never muched liked going to town, and this period away from their home having treatment was difficult. When they got back to Yea, he decided no more. No more trips to Melbourne. He was checked into Yea hospital and from there, into Rosebank aged-care facility. They had a hostel wing, and Lorraine moved in the first chance she got. There was no point being at the house without him. It wasn't home without Ken.

For weeks, Lorraine walked to his bedside from her wing and sat there holding his hand. One time he patted the bed beside him and said she was there, but she wasn't *there*. Lorraine said there was plenty of room in her king single bed, but it wasn't to be. No more nights in her arms. On another day, he rued that they never got to eat together. Off Lorraine went to plan a date night in the dining room for the following day. The staff said they'd arrange a special spot for the two of them, with flowers on the table. They would set the table real nice.

They never had their date. Ken fell asleep the night before and never woke up again.

Ken didn't see the town come out for his funeral. He didn't see the street blocked off for the parade of cars to the cemetery. He didn't hear the president of the RSL say that if it wasn't for Ken's dedication and work, the club would never have seen its one hundredth anniversary. He didn't see the fire brigade, the police, the local business folk or the MP, all standing there in his honour. But Yea did see it, Ken. Well done, mate.

In memory of Kenneth James Howson
18/12/1933–22/11/2019

HH

The Wiliest Fox
There Ever Was

Trudy and David desperately wanted kids and had been trying all the usual ways, but it just wasn't happening. Luckily, their three Labradors ('because everything else is just a dog') helped offset their hankerings. There was Jaguar, the retired police Labrador (David was a copper for twenty-eight years), and two rescue Labradors, Pippa and Bandit.

Canberra became home when Trudy earnt a job in the capital's Health Department and the lovebirds quickly established a new life they were happy with. They loved each other to bits and pieces and had their three furry kids, who loved them back in spades. Trudy and David's daily walk together at the local park was jointly cherished. Plus, back at home, Trudy was a beast in the kitchen, so they also loved their chicken pie and chocolate mousse. All the good stuff. They weren't the big-life types. A little, love-filled life was plenty enough for them.

One random weekday, down at their local park, a short, almost frumpy old lady appeared with a chocolate Labrador, holding one of those scooper, ball-thrower stick things, a nice bright red one. She appeared to be in her mid-sixties and looked like everybody's favourite grandma. She and her chocolate Labrador loved playing ball together. Fortuitously, Trudy and David's chocolate Labrador, Bandit, also happened to love playing ball. The four Labradors became firm playmates and, unsurprisingly, their boundlessness birthed a rich kinship between the three adult neighbours.

They started chatting, but so thick was her accent that Trudy and David initially didn't catch much more than her name – Genna. One thing was clear when she spoke: her demeanour was unlike any Trudy and David had ever seen before. Genna was supremely calm. She said little, but when she did her words had meaning. There was such a profound peacefulness to her. An indisputable kindness also shone from her eyes. Her eyes weren't old at all. They were young, with a hint of knowing, and contained a suggestion of something more. A lot more.

Genna became a regular talking point between Trudy and David. They were intrigued by her unique bearing. They'd seen her umpteen times before, she lived on the same street, but they'd never given her more than a cursory smile as they crossed paths. She was just that little old lady who kept to herself. That night, Trudy and David realised they'd erred in being so unthinking about their neighbour. She had a story. Her eyes showed that much. She had seen a lot. Who knew how much? Trudy suggested to David that they invite her over for dinner. David shared her enthusiasm.

Genna graciously accepted their invitation, and Trudy opted for her tried and true combo of chicken pie and mousse. Over dinner, Genna shared her story. She started by explaining that her father was a fox. The wiliest fox there ever was.

Genna was from Hungary and she had a hero. Her father. When she was six years old, the Russians invaded. Genna's family rushed aboard a train to the border. It was packed full of families trying to avoid the carnage. Everyone knew to get off the train one stop before the border, to avoid the Russian guards. But Genna's dad was wily. He alighted with his family three stops before the border, unlike everyone else. The Russians were waiting at the next stop and every family on the train was put into slave labour, internment camps or exterminated.

It was the middle of winter, and ice cold. They found a guide, waited until nightfall and swam across the Danube, dodging Russian searchlights. Genna's dad knew there was a refugee camp on the other side and could see lights beyond the shore. After walking all the way around the camp to determine whether it was a trap or true refuge, they entered through the side furthest from the Danube.

Genna and her dad were sent to Denmark. Genna ended up at school, but Danish was too difficult for her to learn, so she had to start with French first, to set her up for Danish. On top of her Hungarian of course.

Many years later, Genna finally found her place in Canberra. By now she had five languages under her belt and no problem at all securing an interpreting job. It took half a lifetime, but she found freedom. That's why she was so peaceful. Because her father, her hero, outfoxed the Russian army.

He was the reason they could all play ball in the park.

And enjoy mousse for dessert.

SJ

Things You Can't Unsee

Simon was twenty-six years old and had been a fireman for a few years when he was working night shift on 8 April 1996. He had recently moved in with his girlfriend, Sally, who fell hard for his values. She loved that he was kind and interesting, but also interested, fully invested; he was the guy who was always happy to help someone move house, or lend whatever he had to those who needed it. A guy who believed you should contribute whenever you can. He wasn't hard on the eye either. Given Simon's job, Sally was used to visiting family and friends alone. That's how it goes for shiftworkers.

Firefighting is a reactive emergency service, so as always, the team kept themselves busy on this April night with mandatory muster, checking appliances and doing occasional drills. Eastern Hill Station (Number 1) was quiet until a call came in just after 10.30 p.m.

Simon and his senior officer, a weapon of a human, raced to their aerial compliance, circa 1970, and made their way to Kew Cottages. It was a beast of a machine, a cherry picker on steroids, and they patiently steered it through the narrow streets and roundabouts – listening to the radio all the while. 'Flames showing', 'people unaccounted for', 'assistance required'. It's always serious when they throw a heap of assets at something.

This wasn't the first time they'd been called out to Kew Cottages, which consisted of a number of specialist disability accommodation buildings. It was known for its old infrastructure and its substandard fire protection system. The patients were locked in of a night and Simon worried about their ability to get out. He knew as he approached the scene that the residents may not have the wherewithal to throw a chair through a window, or to hatch other escape plans. In this time of economic rationalism, the staffing at the facility had been cut. As had funding to the emergency services. When their vehicle came over the hill, Simon saw thriving flames and billowing smoke. He left his feelings in the truck and set to work.

Richmond and Kew stations were already on site. Simon and his senior knew immediately that their vehicle, whose primary purpose was to access height, was not needed for the single-storey building fire. Instead, they donned their BAs (breathing apparatus) and headed to the entry point. Time to find the unaccounted for. Front entry failed, so they headed around the back of unit 31. Just as they were wrangling the locked door, a 'GET OUT' call came through. The fire had changed and was now devouring its way through the roof – a structural collapse was inevitable. They raced to the side of the building, ducking through the tiles and debris that rained down around them.

There was an access point to a non-fire-affected room. To gain visibility, they crouched down under the smoke and headed left. When sweeping a room, firies go clockwise and move in concentric circles towards the middle. It's important to check wardrobes, as people often get disoriented and find themselves entering cupboards instead of exiting doors. Simon monitored the whereabouts of his partner by following the sound of exhalation through the valves on their BAs – think Darth Vader. They kept visuals on each other by shining their torches around, to catch the reflective strips on their outer trousers. It wasn't a large room, so it didn't take them long to find two men huddled on a bed in the corner. Normally, he and his partner would assist a man each, but the men were non-ambulant, non-verbal, dead weight. As they extracted one man, a relieving team went in to retrieve the other fellow.

Simon and his senior took him to the ambos and returned to the building – coverlines were in from the paddocks, the fire was 'knocked down', the building had fallen in on itself. But it was too late to save the lives of nine innocent men whose bodies were piled up on the wrong side of a door – they had tried to clamber out.

Simon had seen dead bodies, from jumpers to car crashes, and he'd gone home upset before. But not like this. He was upset for a long time. This was a helpless and unnecessary situation that resulted in the deaths of those who couldn't help themselves. All those powerless people locked up, incarcerated, in an undermanned, underfunded facility. They'd done nothing wrong.

The man who came home in the early hours after his shift was different. He had an edge that couldn't be softened. Sally says he wouldn't talk – Simon says he didn't know what to say. The helplessness of those people had bewildered him and for whatever reason, the firies couldn't get the job done. This job isn't about wheel alignment quotas or balancing the books – it's about families being a member short. Simon relied on the camaraderie of his colleagues and began drinking with them. A lot.

It was a different era. PTSD and mental health weren't on the general discussion table yet. Staff support was minimal. The willingness to accept assistance was too low. When Simon did his training, the philosophy was to get the young fellas in there early – they were going to have to see it all sometime. It was rare to see someone put up their hand to say they had a bad day. Hard to believe that the old days were as recent as 1996.

Simon married Sally, who stood by him until he got better. He's not sure when that was, but parenting helped. Originally, he planned to stay in the service for five years or so. He's now twenty-nine years into his five-year plan. It's been tough lately, with the media portraying the firies as union thugs, and he has stopped telling new people he meets what he does for a living. There have been too many that espouse nonsense, like the idea that firies earn too much and only work five months a year. But the kids still wave at them, and he takes enormous pride in running into a situation that others are running from – to help people when they're at their lowest ebb.

Simon refers to himself as a crusty old fireman now. Maybe he is. But he keeps an eye out on the young ones. He doesn't rush them headlong into the depths of the job's trauma. He teaches them that they don't have to see what they don't have to see. He tells them the smell will never leave their nostrils, they'll never quite unsee things and sometimes there's not enough time in the equation to do what they need to do. He encourages the up and comers to get help when they need it, no shame in that. He checks in with them and makes himself available for coffee and a chat. It's a sometimes challenging job, but it's rewarding and he loves it. Simon says it's about saving lives, and if it's viable, they all give it a red-hot fucking go.

HH

Pounding the Pavement

Jo had tried running before, but it never took. At forty-two, she tried again. Not to lose weight, not for a purpose, for her.

Whichever direction she took when she stepped outside her front door, it was uphill. The township of Morrisons is in a valley and it provided a beautiful setting for her to get the headspace she craved. It was her time. The kids were old enough to stay at home as she pounded the ground. Before long she hit the 1K mark, then 2 and so on. Her uncle Rob was inspired by her efforts, so he started running too. Separately.

When Jo's father died of cancer, she signed up to run a half marathon in Geelong to raise money for the local cancer centre that had cared for him. Uncle Rob signed up too. Not just for the marathon, but to be there for Jo now her dad was gone. They egged each other on. Jo got the local community involved as well. She told the town that she was running for all the people who had died, not just hers. The locals all donated, and in return they wrote the names of their lost ones on her shirt. The community watched her running up and down the nearby hills, honking their horns as they passed her. Jo is a childcare worker, so all the local kids knew her in some way too. They'd find out she was heading their way and wave her along from the roadside, or from their front windows. Jo's husband, Paul, was often seen riding his bike alongside her.

When Jo ran, she could leave her dead behind her for a little while. Her father, her brother and her childhood friend, Michelle, who she had sat with way back when in the children's hospital.

Jo has since run the Melbourne Marathon twice, again with the names of the lost on her shirt – raising money to help find a cure. Maybe one day there will be less names on her shirts. Each marathon, Paul plants himself somewhere along the way so he can smile and wave at her. She loves seeing his face. And she has expanded her fundraising efforts too. Last year she meticulously planned a trivia night and she couldn't believe it when it sold out. Another 6K for research, and she's full of ideas. She has harnessed her loss, spun it on its head and spat it out into action.

Jo still runs for herself. She intends on finishing five marathons before she turns fifty. But she also runs for us. Not just the people who write names on her shirts, for all of us.

HH

Refuse to Lose

Eldest child Jacqueline, and her younger sisters, Claire and Robyn, shared a nauseatingly stable upbringing. Mum Bryony was a total stunner in her day, according to everyone, and apparently Dad Neil was no slouch in the looks department either. Their life was more than just pretty on the outside, though; it was more beautiful on the inside.

Mum Bryony stayed at home and was hands-on with the kids from the start; she would often be seen down on her knees, or plonked on her bum, right there at ground-level with her girls, and Bryony lovingly nurtured her daughters' natural curiosity with experiential learning. Bryony was a formidable teacher and a quality mother. She certainly did most of the heavy lifting when it came to the actual parenting of the three girls.

Dad Neil was one of those permanently distracted fellows, obsessive about his work, and if not for Mum Bryony's shrewdness, the girls would have never known their father as the twinkly eyed, sneaky, fun-loving character that he was, so lost in his passions was he. Resentment towards Dad's work was forbidden. He was saving many families, and that was more important than one family. Simple. Mum Bryony and the girls got all of Neil once a year, and the Bright family spent every Australia Day weekend on a camping trip with their family friends. These annual camping weekends were sacrosanct, insisted upon and fully administered by Bryony, and provided the three girls with their most cherished memories of their larger-than-life father.

Bryony supported her husband unequivocally and with good reason; he had the goods. So when Neil received a prestigious offer to study important surgeon business in London, she enthusiastically moved her brood across the world. Three years later, upon the completion of his studies, the family returned to Australia, when eldest daughter Jacqueline was ten.

Dad Neil was now a qualified surgeon and planned to establish his own practice in Albury, on the Murray River between Sydney and Melbourne. Jacqueline remembers vividly the vast change in the family's standard of living. These were lean days, but that's not what perturbed Neil. He cared deeply for his patients, and it was the substandard treatments being offered regionally that infuriated him. He decided quickly that the care people received in his region mustn't be inferior to the care offered in the city. It was his non-negotiable. Doing something to bridge that gap consumed Neil for the rest of his days and became his fiercest passion.

Before Neil could advocate for change, he first had to get his practice up and running. In the beginning, it tanked. For quite a time, Neil couldn't afford to pay wages, but his staff believed in what he was trying to do and they stayed with him, unpaid, in good faith. Neil was making a big play from a small place, constantly reinforcing his 'Refuse to Lose' mantra, and his passion was infectious. He was a natural leader and his team were as supportive of him as Bryony. It wasn't just his twinkly eyes. He cared deeply and genuinely for his patients, and that can't be faked. If it were, his team wouldn't have stayed with him. Others were learning, like Bryony had early, that Neil had the goods.

Just as soon as he could, Neil started advocating for a rural clinical school in Albury. There were some existing students in the region as part of their rotation, mostly from the University of New South Wales, but they only did one year of training before scooting back to the city. The skill sets that Neil and his cohorts were developing weren't coming back to the community – there was no return on their investment of time, knowledge and care. Of course, this exacerbated the imbalance in care that Neil was trying to redress. And no way was Neil going to be a part of the problem.

Neil started small with his advocacy work, then gradually brought others along with him to learn, and to then advocate themselves on behalf of the district. Eventually, after navigating the countless hoops that invariably come with bureaucratic change, funding from the government for a rural clinical school in Albury was secured. Neil had corralled his students, patients, colleagues and his community, then collectively cajoled, coerced, appealed and agitated until the problem of inequity was properly addressed.

That little rural medical school started small, with just four students, and grew with Neil as he aged. Neil felt strongly that using video conferences as a teaching method was vastly inadequate and disadvantaged his students, so he secured further funding to bring in actual practitioners to teach alongside him. His 'Refuse to Lose' attitude made Neil the school's perfect custodian, measurable also by the strength of the bonds he shared with his students. That's not to say he was an easy teacher. The best aren't. Many of Neil's students were intimidated by his formidable character, but demanding the best of those around him also garnered him their respect, evidenced by the constancy of social invites.

Once the clinical school and his practice was secured he and his group of advocates started working for a Border Cancer Centre. Neil supervised the first Whipple surgery (pancreaticoduodenectomy, an operation to remove tumours from the pancreas) in Australia. Around this time his daughter Jacqueline was starting to realise that her dad was more than a surgeon. She couldn't have lunch with her dad without some random rushing in and thanking him for saving their life. It seemed to happen everywhere they went.

Neil loved teasing his daughters and he often told them he was going to live to 110 so he could help with the great-grandchildren and annoy them forever. He had such an indefatigable attitude, it became easy to believe. Which led to quite the shock when Neil was diagnosed with a deadly cancer himself, and promptly placed in the very Border Cancer Centre he'd help establish.

After news of his diagnosis spread, an exhibition was organised, to sell prints of Neil's travel photography, to raise some cash for the Border Cancer Centre. Sisters Jacqueline, Claire and Robyn, and Mum Bryony couldn't believe how many people came. The place was packed and people came from all corners. Many guests had come from interstate, others had driven hundreds of kilometres. It was on that night – as every print sold instantly, as Neil discussed dissertations with existing students and was greeted by all he'd assisted in his distant past – that Neil's girls realised just how special their dad was. They knew he was special, but they didn't quite know how important he was to others. He was treated like some kind of god. Neil unknowingly delivered his own eulogy that night, and died three days later. At the time of his death, fifty-four students had graduated from the rural medical school he'd helped build.

The funeral was bigger than the exhibition. It again left the girls with a profound sense of their father's greatness. But while Neil was a hero to many (he was awarded an OAM), if you ask his family, they'll tell you that the students and colleagues who supported their dad through his illness are the true heroes, for making Neil's last days so memorable.

Jacqueline is a strategic planner – she plans long-term change, bushfire mitigation and land management. Robyn works in project and change management for the wealth sector. Claire is an environmental scientist, working for local government. The daughters are delivering, in real terms, on their promise to uphold their dad's 'Refuse to Lose' legacy. Big shoes filled.

SJ

When Heroes Collide

Alison is the principal of an outer-suburban secondary college, a big school with a constantly shifting, licorice allsorts student body. Alison has long been concerned with others. After finishing her Dip. Ed. in psychology, Alison was encouraged into a placement with adult male survivors of sexual abuse. It was a case of 'too much, too soon' for the young grad, and Alison pivoted into education, where she happily remains to this day.

Alison, while attentive to the needs of all her students, focuses particularly on the young kids mucking up. The kids no one wants to teach. Some kids have to jump through fifteen hoops just to arrive at school, never mind with the right uniform and a packed lunch. Nobody talks about these kids much. It's easier to showcase the dux of a school, or to boast of grade averages. Difficult kids get moved around; performance outcomes override welfare and learning sometimes. Not for Alison. Not at her school. As far as she's concerned, send all those kids her way. She'll pick 'em up and dust 'em off, no drama.

Paige was by far the most challenging student Alison had encountered in all her years. Paige was feisty as fuck, five foot nothing, and harboured all the rage. Rejected by her blood family, with seven siblings who never tried to find her, there was a lot for Paige to be upset about. She was so sad and clearly very angry, but something special shone through her defiance. Alison believed in her. Unequivocally. This was most inconvenient for Paige. No matter how many times Paige told Alison to go fuck herself, Alison kept coming back. Alison wouldn't last, like everyone else, and Paige would prove it with all her fury.

Alison couldn't find any information on this tempestuous young soul who lobbed into her school one day. No papers. No birth certificate. DHS had nothing. After a series of dead-ends, Alison eventually put enough pieces together herself, and suddenly Paige went from thinking she was thirteen to being told by Alison she was in fact fifteen. Alison bought Paige hair extensions that day to help make her feel better. Paige was wise to her, but took the extensions anyway because fuck her. How could someone just take two years from her like that? No home, no life to speak of and now no real time anymore.

Paige figured that if she stuck around too long Alison would tire of her, just like everyone else. But if she acted out and got moved on, it might help her somehow hold on to Alison. So Paige ran away from the college and the foster home, and was subsequently shunted from one 'Ressie' (Residential Care Unit) to another. None worked out. From the moment Paige left Alison, she didn't attend another full day at school. However, Paige found that no matter where she ended up, or how fucked things were, Alison kept caring. She called Paige almost every day. Alison would visit Paige whenever possible, even if just to hand her a shitty Easter egg, or share a hot chocolate. Paige still told Alison to get fucked all the time, but she was softening. Alison was proving that she wasn't like the rest. That she'd never quit on her.

Eventually, after much tumult, Paige found a Ressie which she actually loved. Finally, at sixteen, her first real taste of home. The caseworkers didn't suck, and were genuinely invested in her wellbeing, and every kid in the unit got along really well. She now had friends she cared about. Plus, it was back within a stone's throw from Alison's college, so pretty soon she had Alison bugging her all the time in person again. Life, for the first time in Paige's experience, was looking pretty sweet.

Right at the time Paige was finding some peace, happiness and her first hint of home, DHS told her she had to move again. Not this time. Not without a fight. Paige had Alison at her flank now. Alison and Paige campaigned vigorously, collecting numerous letters of support from her school, caseworkers and peers. Their case was clear. Do not move Paige. Her current situation is working for her.

Eleven people who had never spent any real time with Paige decided she'd be better off in a 'therapy unit', where she could better learn about her own culture. This broke Paige. It was the ultimate and final humiliation. She ran away back to her old Ressie every day for a while before eventually sliding into a full-blown ice habit and two suicide attempts. She really didn't care now. She wasn't embarrassed to be on ice. She didn't give a shit how she looked. She was going to end up dead or in jail. They were her only two possible destinations. It was all fucked. Just totally fucked.

Anyone who has done ice knows how dark it gets. Those who haven't can merely bear witness to the wastage and imagine what lies between. Needless to say, Paige's fury found fire … that dark fire that so few emerge from.

When Paige woke up from her second overdose, she again found Alison by her bedside, telling her she looked like a dead zombie. This time, Alison took Paige back to her house, for a good night's rest on the couch.

It wasn't that Paige stayed, it was more that Paige couldn't leave, especially after Alison bought her a dog to love with all her heart. Between walking her new ball of love, Paige mostly sat on the couch surrounded by new siblings, and had TV and snacks and other good, small things. Paige stopped taking her toiletries out of the bathroom every time she finished in there. She stopped panicking if her phone wasn't right beside her. It was okay for her phone to just sit on the table – no one would steal it. Paige describes this stage on Alison's couch as 'all weird and normal'. Slowly, with normalcy and routine, and a steady flow of TLC, Paige started feeling better. Five months later Paige was well enough to score a job at Macca's. Then, after saving well, Paige took a trip to Noosa and had a great time. A clean time.

* * *

Paige and Alison still fight, and still tell each other to 'go fuck yourself', make no mistake. Paige is still far from okay and knows she will carry her scars to the grave with her. She might not be 'fixed', or 'better', but one thing has changed for certain. Now Paige knows that Alison will never leave her. And that she deserves love. Through sheer dogged persistence, Alison has helped Paige rediscover her courage.

Paige is courageous enough to be ambitious now. She's still all furious and fiery about the residential care system, but she's more measured now, and is determined to become a Ressie worker herself. To be there for the other kidlets who harbour all the fury. She also wants to advocate for change, for DHS to be better funded, with better training for its workers, and she's already given two keynotes on the topic. Paige laughs when she tells me that now *she's* going to annoy the shit out of all the kids, just like Alison did to her!

Not a bad outlook for a seventeen-year-old who's been through the wringer.

SJ

Table of Dignity

Kon's father, Leo, fancied himself becoming a doctor when he grew up, but his parents were extremely poor and Leo was pulled out of school at nine to work the fields. Kon's mother, Sia, dreamt of being a maths teacher, but her parents were poor too, and she was switched into the same fields at twelve. When Leo and Sia fell in love as young adults, they pledged to break the cycle of poverty and hustled their way from Greece to Australia as immigrants in the 1960s, carrying not much English, a suitcase of sacrifices, and the commonly held migrant dream to return home with plenty.

Kon was born in Albury Hospital in 1972 and was raised in nearby Mount Beauty, a little country town of about 1500 people. Kon grew up as one of only two Greek families in the region. Kon's dad, Leo, was a tobacco farmer, out by 5 a.m. and not back until after 9 p.m. Kon will never forget his dad's deeply stained hands. No amount of washing could remove the tobacco.

In 1985 Leo and Sia took a punt and moved to Melbourne in search of more for their kids (bullying was a major issue for both children in Mount Beauty). Leo and Sia were both able to secure factory work – Leo in an asbestos-ridden factory in Collingwood, and Sia in a sock factory in East Brunswick.

Yarra Falls, the factory in Collingwood where Leo worked as a wool bleacher, was Dickensian in its bleak blend of bricks, dust and soot. Except for Leo's garden, that is. There, in the middle of a smudgy industrial wasteland, lay a little patch of defiant beauty: a small, rectangular garden, built and lovingly tended to by Leo, the Greek Montgomery Clift.

Sia was no less charismatic. She sported beautiful thick black hair, like Sophia Loren, an angelic face, and was as well known for her industriousness over at the sock factory as Leo was for his fresh bulbs and cuttings.

Under the surface, things were far more brutal. Kon grew up in extreme poverty. Life was very tough for Sia and Leo; they worked like animals. Every day, Kon's parents traded their aspirations and potential to work in jobs where they were demeaned, mocked and disrespected; all so Kon and his sister could enjoy the relative luxury of attending school. Sia worked at the sock factory until her hands broke. Leo busted a gut, then some. There was a lot of sadness. Sia and Leo may not have achieved their own aspirations of becoming a maths teacher and a doctor, but they would be damned if their kids would be similarly deprived. However bleak things were, Kon's parents always somehow seemed to find beauty amid the darkness. Kon and his sister, Nola, were never without hope. But his parents' sacrifices weighed heavily on them. They didn't want success in their lives to come at the cost of their parents' aspirations.

During their university studies Kon and Nola saved every penny they could gather to pay for their heroes to return home – Leo and Sia hadn't seen Greece for decades and Kon and Nola felt that a trip home was the least they could arrange, as thanks for the sacrifices their parents had made for them. Leo had a heart attack while he was back in Greece and died in his homeland. He never would have the chance to fully enjoy retirement, to stop worrying about the next dollar, to see both his Aussie kids flourish into adults without deep-stained hands.

Since his father's death Kon has spent his life paying tribute to his parents by helping other new migrants transition into life in Australia. And he's used what he calls 'radical empathy' to fuel his efforts. For twenty-nine years,

Kon has shared his story with all and sundry, in an effort to teach people about the typical migrant story: the loss of freedom, the loss of security, the loss of food, the loss of family, and the fear all the loss fosters along with the grief of never being able to return home with plenty. Kon asks the same thing of every person he speaks with. He asks for their empathy. He asks that they treat others as they would treat their own family. He asks for their positivity, and he asks using positivity. He asks that they acknowledge how easy it is to tear things apart and encourages them towards values-based leadership instead. He reminds people that the question of 'what they are doing for others' is the most urgent question in life. He encourages people to do something positive with their anger and disillusionment, to drink from the cup of empathy and welcome to this country new arrivals who, in his words, deserve a seat at the table of dignity.

People have listened to Kon and they've responded on an epic scale. Kon is the proud founder and chief custodian of the Asylum Seeker Resource Centre, which provides support to every new arrival in Victoria, whether it be through the centre's food warehouse and mobile food banks, their employment centre, legal service, entrepreneurial hub, medical centre or accommodation support unit. Kon has over 200 people on staff, most of them migrants themselves, and over 1500 volunteers who are responsible for the bulk of operational duties. It costs about $15 million a year to operate the resource centre, and it is funded almost entirely by community donations.

When COVID-19 hit Melbourne, Kon built a food warehouse in Sunshine, in the city's west, within forty-eight hours. He didn't worry about resourcing – he had faith that his community would have his back. The warehouse was quickly filled with food: row upon row of basmati rice, thousands of tins of beans and tomatoes. Since then, Kon has provided 6000 facemasks, 1000 bottles of hand sanitiser and nearly 5000 culturally appropriate meals to the new arrivals under army supervision in the housing commission estates of Flemington.

* * *

Kon's dad, Leo, built a garden in the middle of one of Melbourne's filthiest factories. Leo offered his bulbs and cuttings to passers-by from his small, defiant rectangle of love. And now Kon tends to his own garden of plenty – his huge, rectangular warehouse of love in Sunshine – that provides, through its food banks, fresh meals for new arrivals at the table of dignity.

SJ

Out the Other Side

Amanda reckons her dad is just terrific. Not that life was always easy. Her dad, Malcolm, is a Vietnam vet and he was very strict when she was little. Most of the dads in the area were vets. Most of their dads' dads were too. Malcolm grew up in Coolah, which means valley of the winds. It was a wool town, and if you didn't want to be a shearer you joined the army, where you were able to learn a trade. The local kids saw some peculiar behaviours from their returned vet dads. One dad would sit out on the street to keep watch over the neighbourhood at night, and at the end of these non-rostered shifts, he would call out 'up the red rooster' – in reference to his squad's mascot. Kids like Amanda had a sense that their dads carried a burden, and she's chuffed that hers paid it forward.

Before Malcolm signed up, he had proposed to the love of his life, Di. He went to Vietnam and married his sweetheart on return. Army life involved uprooting the family. A lot. The whole family spent a couple of years in Papua New Guinea, where Malcolm's vertical construction skills helped him help the locals construct office buildings, hospitals and schools. Despite the 'here and there' nature of the army, he loved it, because he got to work with his mates.

When Malcolm retired in 2008, he decided to delve into himself. He knew he hadn't been easy to live with. That he had a short fuse. There were quiet patches too. Patches where his family couldn't reach him. He had his strategies to deal with his moods – all vets did. Some drank, some threw themselves into their work, and some, like Malcolm, ran ... and ran. There was an awareness of the effect he was having on others. He acknowledges he was autocratic and a burden on his colleagues, and his family had suffered along the way. He knew that he hadn't seen the problems in the same way the people around him had; the people who had adjusted their behaviours to accommodate him. He stopped and looked around. Reflected on past patterns. Malcolm decided it was time to face his PTSD. He sought counselling and after much reluctance, started taking 'a happy pill' once a day. He still keeps up with his psychologist, accepts who he was, who he is, and uses his self-awareness to help others going through the same thing.

These days, Malcolm proudly represents the Castle Hill RSL sub-branch. His specialty is going to see the vets in hospital. Vets who are either physically unwell, or their mental health simply got the better of them. From there he takes note of what further services can be utilised and he steers them in the right direction. Malcolm knows firsthand how valuable these services are. More than that, though, he provides a stellar set of listening ears.

Then there are the side projects. He and his team have found much-needed housing for numerous homeless vets. Malcolm scurries about and finds old unwanted furniture, then uses his carpentry skills to get them up to scratch for their new owners.

He has focused on getting himself right, so he can help others get themselves right. He's keen on helping war vets' wives and widows too. He keeps a close eye on them, because they are inevitably the carers of our vets, and if they crack under pressure the problems double. When they lose their partners, Malcolm makes sure they have enough to get by, and if losing the war pension means losing financial support, he points them in the right direction. To get help. And, of course, he couldn't have got through these years, his PTSD, and being able to help other vets without his sweetheart. He thinks Di is just terrific.

Di acknowledges that the man who came home from Vietnam was not the same as the man she got engaged to all those years ago. Before he left, he was young and carefree, easygoing, calm and lovable. Sure, he was still those things when he got back, but there was an edge that he didn't have before he left. She understood there are things our vets never want to talk about, but Di was in for the long haul. She admires Malcolm for getting the counselling he needed, and they've done some counselling together too. She knows Malcolm has seen so much and that he'll never really forget it. When they go out for dinner, she doesn't mind sitting with her back to the door; she understands he's still on alert. He's a good man who loves a chat and will do anything for anybody, and she does her bit too.

Di, along with Malcolm, is also part of the same RSL sub-branch, and she puts together care packages to be sent overseas – to the next generation of vets. The beanies and scarves they make also go to local homeless people, and just as Malcolm tinkers with furniture to go in the new homes for previously homeless vets, she sources linens and the small things needed to make a house a home.

Di thinks daughter Amanda is just terrific. When she had her childcare centre, there were plenty of kids with issues who passed through her doors. Kids who had been placed nearby with their mums after running from domestic violence. One such boy was also autistic, and he found Amanda particularly calming. His mum would call sometimes, saying she just couldn't get him to settle. Amanda never thought twice about heading over to their place to help out, regardless of the time or day. She also waived fees for a family who had lost their home in a fire, and bought them groceries each fortnight.

This is a family where each person goes over and above. Quietly. A family with a strong work ethic. A belief that you should do what you can, when you can. A family that thinks each other is just terrific for lending a helping hand when someone in the community is in a spot of bother. Because their community is family too.

HH

49 Not Out

Alex has always had a deep-throated cackle and a twinkle in her eye. She was eighteen when she fell pregnant, and the father of the child wanted nothing to do with them once he heard the news. Alex was stoic, even when she was young, so she packed up and moved to Queensland to be near her mum. She delighted in the responsibilities that come with being a young mum and got on with life. She found love again, got married and bought a home.

When her son, Daniel, was three, her knee began to ache. The doctor told her it couldn't be serious because sarcoma tumours only occur in young girls or older women. Alex knew something was wrong, though, so she insisted on a referral to a specialist to try to get to the bottom of her bothersome knee. One day the pain was so bad she took herself off to hospital. Her knee was so hot her husband could barely touch it, and still the doctor inferred that the pain couldn't be as bad as she was claiming.

Three months later, after knocking on more doors, she underwent exploratory surgery to hopefully solve the knee mystery. It was osteosarcoma; and treatment needed to begin immediately. When she arrived for her first chemo session, the new doctor was surprised to see her walking on her leg at all. Alex explained she was keeping up her prescribed exercises to regain strength in the knee. As it turned out, she shouldn't have been exercising at all. There was so much damage to her knee that her leg was being held together by a splinter of bone. A replacement was ordered posthaste.

The next fourteen months involved a whole lot of chemo sessions, a failed knee replacement, a case of gangrene and a dropped foot. Alex walked through all this, carting her largely useless leg around behind her. It felt dead. There were other stresses during this time. She had to give up work; Alex and her husband needed to sell the house as they couldn't make the repayments and he crumbled under the pressure of it all. He couldn't do the things they needed to do as a couple because he was crippled by the weight of their circumstance. She packed for herself and son Daniel and went to stay at her mum's house, to give him some relief from the day-to-day cancer drudgery. The relationship didn't survive – sometimes love isn't enough. So Alex got on with it. She took charge and moved on; dead leg in tow. These times weren't all hard. She felt loved and supported, and she made a swag of new friends who she met in her support groups. Her throaty cackle got many work-outs between hospital visits.

At the conclusion of her chemo, the doctors suggested an amputation. Alex thought 'thank god' because she was sick of carting that leg around. Next St Patrick's Day, her leg was amputated. She had an electric wheelchair and was looking forward to getting her prosthetic leg, when she was told she was going to have to wait. The Adriamycin in her chemo regime had left her heart muscles so damaged she was given just twelve months to live.

Again, Alex got on with things. Off she went to see a lawyer and Daniel was placed in her mother's custody. She needed to know he was going to be safe after she died. This period saw her strangely calm. She started a range of medications for her 'heart thing', she went on a trip to Sydney to see *The Phantom of the Opera* with her mum (thanks to Make a Wish), and she continued her regular appointments. At one of these appointments, she found a perplexed cardiologist. Her health was improving. The cardiologist was more surprised than she was, and he informed her she just might make forty. She got that prosthetic leg, packed Daniel and herself up and moved back to Melbourne to spend time with the rest of her family.

Alex found another love, remarried and embraced life. Perhaps a little too much. There was binge drinking and partying. She would get so drunk that she would get angry, break things and contemplate suicide. This was the hard period for Daniel. When she had been going through treatment when he was young, he didn't go to the hospital often. He went to day care and school and socialised and did kid things. This next period, now that he was a little older, was not so idyllic, but they got through it together. Alex says she went a 'bit nutty' for ten years. She came to realise she wasn't well mentally. She took herself off for counselling and gave up the grog. She worked hard and now she knows what to do with her feelings. She can see the warning signs, she knows when to take herself out of things for a day or two and no longer suffers psychotic episodes. The unexpected milestone of turning forty was celebrated with a big, binge-drinking-free affair. Alex felt the worst was behind her.

When Daniel was twenty-one, he was a passenger in a horrendous car accident. He was airlifted to hospital and underwent months of rehabilitation. Alex's second husband couldn't deal with the stress and said he couldn't support her. So she left him and sat by her son's side. Her health took a turn from the worry. She believes the stress caused her diabetes, so she took charge. By hook or by crook she was going to be there for her son, despite her heart function now being down to 20 per cent. She took really good care of herself so she could take really good care of Daniel, who now had a new hip. The dynamic duo. Daniel, like his mother, had married young and his wife's family lived back in Queensland. After his recovery, the young couple wanted to move to her homeland to raise their future babies. Alex was not going to be left behind. She packed herself, Daniel and his wife up and off they went. Daniel had a daughter, and Alex relaxed into her new family life.

After a while, Alex's arm would go numb and she would wake in the night with a sore neck. Off to the doctor again. Her neck was clear, but the scans showed tumours in her right breast and right lung. After a lumpectomy and some radiation, it was decided her heart was too weak for chemo. She couldn't have medical oxygen due to her weak heart, so the usual surgical options were not available for Alex. It also meant that when they had to cut her amputated leg down further and place a new muscle flap on her stump, an epidural was the best they could offer for the duration of the operation. Doctors told her she may make her forty-fifth birthday.

None of this has deterred Alex from enjoying her life, her family and sunny Queensland. She knows the cancer or the heart will get her, and that's just how it is. She's getting on with it.

'Well I'm forty-nine now and I'm going to make fifty,' she said, with a throaty cackle. 'They've been telling me I have twelve months to live for the last twenty years!' The cancers haven't diminished her laughter. 'And then I'm going to set my sights on seeing my new grandson on his first day of school in four and a half years.'

Well, Alex, we fervently hope you are there to see the young fella walk through those gates. God speed.

HH

Taking it Back

There can come a time when even the hardiest of optimists lose all hope.

It's not quite so scary to people who feel hopeless often, because it's at least a familiar feeling for them. But if one truly loses hope, having never lost it before, well, that's a mighty fall.

Natalie was known to all as an unshakable optimist, just like her dad. She was the youngest, Daddy's little girl. She had a classic 'play on the streets until dark' upbringing and loved tagging after her brother who caught lizards and knew all the goat tracks.

When puberty and young adulthood hit, Natalie strung

together a series of typical teenage errors. Her father never came down hard on her, only ever providing reassurance, as he too remembered what it was like to be young. It wasn't her fault; making mistakes was just part of growing up.

Natalie always wanted a family, and to work in early childhood education like her mum. At a very young age she knew, deep inside her heart, that only she would pave that future. They were her two immutable truths: she would be a great parent, just like hers were, and she would achieve all of her ambitions and more. Her confidence didn't allow for a Plan B. Why would it? When she knew everything would work out just fine!

And it did. Natalie found just about the only fella in the district who shared her dad's calibre, and they went about building their dreams together. They built everything they ever wanted. And it went beautifully. Their optimism led to outcomes that were, well … optimistic.

When their kids were four, seven and twelve, Natalie became tired. That wasn't in her repertoire, so she saw a doc and was eventually told she had cancer. When the diagnosis finally dropped, Natalie responded with her customary optimism and got on with it. No use wallowing. She didn't tell her family. Their business didn't give a hoot about cancer and her kids still needed her. Although she didn't know it at the time, she was starting to play tricks on herself. Her denial started to serve as a shield against a painful, pessimistic truth.

She buried herself in her work until it became obsessive. She finally told her family about the cancer, but dismissed the seriousness of the situation. After a particularly nasty surgery, she was doing payroll in her hospital bed within hours of waking up. She *needed* this and wouldn't be deterred. No matter what. Natalie was neglecting herself. Her work wouldn't shield her forever. She had to find a way to stop.

The stress she was placing herself under was real, and she was using her work to distract herself from the truth. She was 'faking it till she made it' on the outside, while it was slowly crippling her on the inside.

Natalie got tired again. She knew without being told. The cancer was back. She was rushed back into surgery and after another major operation, her surgeon was anything but optimistic.

That's when it happened. That's when Natalie's hope simply vanished. She couldn't think properly. She couldn't function. Her mind was broken. She was broken. She fell apart. Completely.

It was then that her family intervened. They had been seriously worried for some time. Natalie's sister told her there was no shame in talking to someone, and admitting her fears.

A therapist would help. The therapist suggested Natalie regain some of the control she felt she had lost. Reassess. Why not quit her job and change her life completely? 'Big call,' thought Natalie, as she left that particular session. But she couldn't argue, really.

Then the shame hit. Shame that the cancer had broken her. Shame that cancer had taken the one thing she had left: her trademark optimism. Her family and friends reached out but she didn't know how to function without that piece of herself. She tried to protect others from her pain by shutting them out completely. She went alone, to the place with no hope.

Natalie came out the other side changed. She looked at her life and none of it made sense. She didn't want anything anymore. It all seemed to mean nothing. All that work, for what? Without her distractions she felt worthless. And when cancer takes everything, you learn that there is only ever one thing that remains. Family.

So she took control again. She quit her job and started to rid herself of all superfluous material possessions, accepting that they held very little significance in her life. Natalie and her hubby packed their kids and their life into a van and they just set off. Left it all behind. No plans, no expectations, other than simply being together. Together in precious moments.

Natalie has been on the road with her brood for nine months now. She's back at work, although remotely this time, supporting her hubby. She's healthy, but she knows that may not be forever and she's okay with that. She's still rebuilding, but once again, after a good long while, her optimism is back and her days are bright.

SJ

Dipped in Gold

Bribbaree is a small town in New South Wales that stands on the edge of the Hilltops Region, at the beginning of the Great Western Ranges. Bribbaree is the classic, proverbial dot on the map. Many in the region couldn't point you towards it. The nearest supermarket is a 35-minute drive away in Young, to the west. Bribbaree boasts a population of thirty, give or take. There's a wonderful old pub, a lawn bowling club, showgrounds, a memorial hall and a servo, and that's about it. The town has seen better days, a lack of people being the main issue.

Pat is a Bribbaree girl, born and bred, although she spent thirty years at the Department of Education in Canberra, first in a typing pool, then in facilities management, before returning home to enjoy her twilight years. Upon return she bought a farm. Many locals doubted her ability to farm; suffice to say they're coming around.

Pat keeps herself in good nick, and always dresses impeccably. Once, her son-in-law went to leave the house in trackies. 'You're not going down to the shops looking like that.' Which he met with, 'I'm going to get the paper, not to a job interview.'

While Pat's hubby drove trucks and was away on long runs, Pat did her share of heavy haulage back home, raising two nippers and putting herself through evening school and community college, qualifying as a wool classer and silversmith. Pat was a single mum during the week, married on weekends, and she was known to never complain. When Pat's father fell terminally ill she was there by his side the whole way. Afterwards, Pat's daughter Mandi remembers asking her mum if she was coping okay.

'It was an honour, not a burden,' was Pat's response.

Pat started the after-school care program at her kids' school. In 1991 she was recognised by the government for her work in the education sector and in 2003 she was part of the security team that was set up after the Canberra fires. Of all her work, Pat is perhaps proudest of her achievements on the regional Bribbaree Showgrounds, though she'd never boast of it, of course.

When Pat took over the Bribbaree Show Society there was $5K in the cheque account and a lot of improvements to be made. Of course, in Pat's world, if there's a problem, you fix it yourself, or have it fixed. Before you could say 'Bribbaree Showgrounds' Pat went through the place like a dose of salts. New seating. New barbeque area. New colour schemes. New processes, top to bottom. Simultaneously, she was dreaming of a new pavilion and familiarising herself with the local grants schemes.

Pat learnt that $50K would get Bribbaree a lovely new pavilion and before long she had secured $40K from the government – but they were $10K short. Pat wrote to GrainCorp and secured the remaining $10K. After it was built, despite her wishes, it was named the Pat Potbury Pavilion.

It used to be that the Bribbaree Showgrounds had one show day per calendar year. Now there's also a Stockman's Challenge and a Show and Shine car show. And there's more to come.

Pat isn't on the Show Society Committee anymore, but she's still a part of the Showgrounds Management Trust. She has recently secured a further $134K, for more improvements. Rumour has it that the Bribbaree

Showgrounds will be dipped in gold by the time Pat is all said and done.

Bribbaree, population thirty, give or take, may always be a proverbial dot on the map. But, thanks to Pat, it's a very shiny dot.

SJ

The Karate Kid

Heather had an appointment at four o'clock that day, to find out whether she had cancer or not. But it wasn't foremost on her mind. As she was getting ready for work, she walked around the whole house and woke up the young adults strewn about the place. She was looking for her son, Shannon. She wanted to remind him about his driving lesson that afternoon. His twin brother was home, as were all the friends Shannon had gone out with the night before. Heather's house was always at capacity. If there were no beds left, anyone was welcome to some floor.

When Heather was eighteen, her life was uprooted. She followed her family to Mildura, as her father had found a good job there. She didn't want to leave Melbourne, her life, her friends, but it was what it was. And it was hot. She went to the pool and met a local lad, David, who was most passionate about springboard diving. There wasn't a great future for him in Mildura, and as love blossomed, the two of them moved to Melbourne so he could pursue his diving career; and Heather could return to her life.

Although Heather had wanted to work in a zoo, she openly admits she didn't have the wherewithal to do the required study. Instead, she set up home with David and turned their outer-east home into a menagerie. David gave diving a red-hot go, and even made the World Masters at twenty-five. They had jobs: Heather at a bank and David at Telecom, and they planned to buy a house of their own. They married, and when they were twenty-nine, twin boys came along – out of the blue. Heather had never much cared for travel, she was happy in their home with their menagerie, and they doted on their boys. There were family trips back to Mildura, and they had no regrets about not travelling the world. They were happy.

The twins weren't identical, and they had different interests. Heather loved that Shannon was eighteen years old, yet still went to karate classes with his mother. Kids that age don't usually embrace activities with their mum, and

Heather enjoyed making her way through the karate ranks with him. They even did competitions together.

Heather was worried when Shannon was nowhere to be seen, but she told herself that eighteen-year-olds have their own lives and do their own things, so she took herself off to work at the bank. She phoned home in her breaks, but still there was no Shannon. When she went to her medical appointment, she was told she had cancer. She heard the doctor talking of treatments and laying out battle plans to fight it, but she didn't listen. All she could think about was Shannon.

When she got home, she told the family about her results – except for Shannon. She walked to the supermarket after tea with her husband, they liked taking strolls together, and on the way home, dog food in hand, Heather suggested they pop into the police station. They agreed the police would think they were overreacting, but they'd watched enough telly to know that they could file a missing person report. When they got there, they told the nice man at the counter that their son was missing, and they were ushered into an interview room. Heather was thrilled that they were taking her seriously. Another nice man came in and sat down – he wasn't in uniform. He told them that a young man matching Shannon's description had been found at the local soccer ground in the early hours. He had hanged himself. Heather just sat there. She didn't even cry. Her body couldn't process it.

But her brain was in overdrive. What if they'd slept with the bedroom door open, maybe she would have heard him leaving? She pictured him walking past all of them that night. What if he was stressed about her cancer – was the idea of his mum being sick too much for him? What signs had she missed? But he had so many friends, didn't he?

Heather went looking for answers over the next while but couldn't find any. Her doctor said, 'Heather, sometimes people just take their own lives.' Heather still has no answers, and she knows she never will.

Shannon's funeral was full of the people who loved him. Seven hundred kids came, yet he had felt so alone. He was the friend that others turned to. The one who gave sage advice on life's turmoils. His friends said things like 'he always cheered me up' and 'he understood others' pain'. His friends still visit Heather, and she values their time. There was a girl in the house that night. A girl Shannon cared about. A girl who came to Heather's home a few days after the funeral and broke down on the doorstep. But didn't come inside. Heather has messaged her on Facebook, but they've never talked. Grief has a long reach.

For a while, Heather didn't want to walk the local streets. Everyone knows she's the woman with cancer whose son suicided. She feels that all the eyes are on her. That no one knows what to say. And when they do say something, they always ask about her cancer. They never mention Shannon. No one asks how she's coping with his death. Heather calls it the silent epidemic. Everyone talks about the road toll, about cancer. But the emotional cost of suicide is silent. Heather doesn't know what to do about this, because she's read that discussion may lead to others doing the same thing. That it comes in clusters. She doesn't want to make a noise in case this is true, but she wants to shout it from the rooftops. She wants it on the table. What if it led to one less death? What if it's not contagious after all, and her story could prevent one other family from going through this?

Heather went skydiving for Shannon on his twenty-first birthday. And she still goes to karate. She's about to go for her brown belt, without him, with him, for him.

HH

More Than a Pharmacist

Fahim, affectionately known to all as Frank, was of short stature and average build. He had a round, friendly head wrapped in caramel brown skin, bald but for a tiny island of hair on the very top of his dome. He loved his little island of hair, and often mocked himself by being overly attentive to it whenever a mirror was near, invariably drawing laughter and a lifting of the mood. Frank's eyes were lively, his teeth were slightly crooked, and together they combined to produce a genuine smile that stood as Frank's most talked-about feature. Frank was a clean-cut gentleman and took pride in his appearance. He wore his preferred dark purple cardigan to work most days, over which he would wear his white pharmacist's apron. This subtle flair was about as extravagant as Frank got, for while he was a fun person, he wasn't showy. Humour and humility were his compound mixes.

Frank grew up in a small town in Lebanon called Blouza, the second of six kids. Chickens and goats punctuate his memories of a small, simple, happy existence. Frank moved to Australia when he was ten years old. His parents drilled him on the importance of education and consequently Frank did well at school, went to Sydney University and became a pharmacist. As he grew older Frank started harbouring a dream: to take his family home to Lebanon during fig season.

Frank's daughter Linda grew up as one of five, and she resented her dad for working so hard. Frank worked six days out of seven and was always too tired to play on Sundays. Frank was, however, always there to listen when his kids needed to talk. Linda mightn't have had the playmate she desired, but she had the father she needed when it came to life stuff. He was a keen listener and always seemed to provide Linda with great insight and tangible advice. This is what Linda loved about her dad, his attentiveness to her.

Fortunately, Frank was able to enjoy a chunk of his retirement before cancer bested him. His funeral was scheduled and announced, and Linda went to her father's service expecting a reasonably sized group of friends and family to attend.

A tsunami of humans flowed in for Frank's funeral service, surprising everyone in the family. Linda was dumbfounded. Linda knew her dad worked with other migrants and helped them with their transitions into Australian life. Linda knew that Frank waived fees and financially supported those within his community experiencing hardship. Linda suspected that Frank was as well loved within his community as he was at home, but she had no concept of her father's reach within that community; no concept of how many people considered her father in high enough regard to attend his service. Stories abounded that day, of the friendly, dignified pharmacist who actually cared and genuinely helped.

Linda's resentment is gone now. Now all Linda wants is to go to Lebanon in fig season, and to find and sit in Blouza, her father's home town, and to attentively recall his stories of chickens and goats, and the simple life.

SJ

To the End of the Desert and Back

Belinda was born and raised in Victoria, but she craved adventure. She crossed the Nullarbor at twenty-seven with her two kids, her husband and her dog – full of plans for their new lives in outback Western Australia. He was going to work in the mines. She was going to look after the kids and do some courses, so she could get a good job when the kids hit school age. When she was tending to one of the children in the back seat, she thought she had knocked her boob. As she settled herself back into the front seat, it was sore. She felt around and found a small lump, but she wasn't worried. They settled into their new life.

Over the next couple of months, she went about her business and called the growing lump her 'third boob'. She went to a few doctors who dismissed it, but eventually she was sent to Perth for a lumpectomy. Belinda's mum flew over to look after the kids and a couple of weeks after surgery, she told her mum it was okay to go back home. There had been no news and they had told her it was most likely a cyst – because only older women get cancer. The same day her mum went to the airport, Belinda got a phone call. She was told it was cancer – a tumour in her milk ducts. Belinda stopped breastfeeding and her husband cried. He was very supportive, and Belinda encouraged him to go back to work while she navigated the medical system. The stress had disabled him, and he was having trouble holding down a job since the news came in.

Belinda blamed the doctors for not finding the cancer earlier. She was meant to be starting a new life, not facing roadblock after roadblock. There was also pressure from her family to return home to Victoria, but Belinda was determined to continue their new lives in their new place.

Her first chemo was booked in on the same day her eldest child started school. She asked the doctors if a delay would kill her. When they said no, she deferred her chemo for a couple of weeks so she could support her young boy through his transition to school. After her chemo rounds finished, she needed to have radiation every day for three weeks; but she was living too remotely for this to be feasible. So she and the children travelled back to Victoria to stay with family. That way she could attend daily treatments with a minimum of fuss. Her husband came to visit and lost another job. When radiation finished, Belinda and the kids returned to WA. If you had walked past Belinda in the street, you wouldn't have seen any signs of her struggles. She has a warm face, free of resentment, and a zest for life.

Belinda became more and more driven and inspired after treatment. Her husband less and less so. Belinda worked at Officeworks while she completed a real estate course. When she began work at a local agency, she completed a course in aged care. While she had cast a wide employment net, her marriage had slowly disintegrated. Her husband still hadn't been able to hold down a job and ended up moving back to Melbourne. But she had no ill will towards him. He had done the best he could under the pressure. Belinda and the kids stayed in WA, she went to her yearly check-ups and after five years, she was given the all-clear. On that day she got a tattoo on her back that read 'courage and determination'. She had also met a new man. Although she wasn't living the life she had planned, she was happy again.

Belinda got married and they went to Bali for their honeymoon. She was twenty weeks pregnant and thrilled that the chemo hadn't taken away her chance to have more children. She was from a large family and looked forward to having a swag of kids herself. While in Bali, she started bleeding and took herself to hospital. She couldn't understand anything the doctors were saying, but she knew they'd lost their child. Her new husband was as devastated as she was, and they returned home early. They went on to have two daughters, but there were cracks in the marriage.

Although Belinda loved the chaos of a big family, her husband had been an only child and became overwhelmed. He also worked long hours and night shift to support her and the four kids. Unbeknownst to Belinda, he was taking substances to stay awake for his long hours. Belinda says people make assumptions about the types of people who find themselves on drugs. It can happen to anyone, and his well-meaning choices to stay awake for work spiralled. When Belinda discovered his drug use, they worked together, and he got clean.

Her husband worked on cars in the yard in his spare time. On one occasion Belinda had a burning sensation on her chest. She assumed he hadn't cleaned his hands properly when he touched her, and some wayward battery acid had found its way to her chest. She ignored the burning sensation, but only for a day. Then she took herself off to the doctor, who dismissed it as mastitis and gave her antibiotics – she wasn't even breastfeeding. Belinda shrugged and continued planning their redo honeymoon. Mum came back over to watch the kids and off they went. In Bali, they saw an old medicine man sitting on a street corner. He was touching and healing people with a metal stick. Belinda smiled as her husband got healed. The old man looked quizzically at her and ushered her over. She wasn't interested, but his gesturing was insistent. He poked and prodded her with his stick for nearly an hour, and Belinda found herself full of foreboding. She shrugged it off and enjoyed the rest of her holiday.

When they got back home, Belinda went off to the doctors again. The feeling of foreboding hadn't diminished. More scans; more cancer. Belinda didn't want to tell her husband. She didn't want him to regress into using again, but she couldn't keep a double mastectomy from him forever. He didn't take the news well and they blundered along under the diagnosis cloud, doing the best they could with the kids. He went to the hospital with her and waited for her while she had the operation. Pre-op she had been asked whether she wanted reconstructive surgery. She said she wasn't too fussed and politely declined. When she woke up, she was looking forward to a hug. Her husband was there, but there was no hug. He said he was tired and went home. Belinda ended up crying in the arms of a nurse. But not for long.

When she felt rested, Belinda wanted to go and have a coffee. She got out her phone to check their bank account. It showed her husband had taken out $200 at an ATM near his old dealer. Belinda didn't get her coffee and recovered alone. She didn't want to fight with him. She wanted to use her energy on herself – so she could get home to her babies. She was done with her marriage, but finances kept them under the same roof for a while. It was during this time that she felt low. She had lost her womanhood, and her husband pointed out that no one would ever want her the way she was now. His words kept whirling around her head. Her body image, which had been fine pre-surgery, had plummeted.

The marriage was over, and Belinda had moved to a rental property half an hour away from the house she had bought with her second husband. He couldn't make the repayments and she had to go to family court to force the selling of the house. She didn't do it for money, there was none, she did it to curb the rising debt. The maintenance man at her work had built up many hours of sick leave over the years, and he donated them to her, with head office permission. Belinda still marvels at his generosity. But this money was long gone, and she could only work spasmodically. Belinda decided it was unfair for her parents to continue flying over to WA to help her. It was time to go home. Her eldest son was seventeen and had already returned to Melbourne to start an apprenticeship. She sold off her furniture and hired a trailer. Belinda, her three daughters, her mum and her old dog made the trip back across the Nullarbor, with a couple of brief roadside stops for a nap.

Belinda is home now. Last July she started another course. She's going to be a breast care nurse. She still goes to hospital for bone infusions, and she will have them for the next five years. These infusions harden the squishy middle of bones, which make the bones unattractive to the cancer cells travelling around her body. She no longer sticks to an organic diet. She wants to enjoy life, and if she feels like a deep-fried chicken wing, she eats a deep-fried chicken wing. But not too often. Belinda looks younger than her age, and the fine lines around her soft eyes are smile lines.

Belinda is struggling through her course as she's not a natural academic. Others in her class get higher marks, but these classmates have also told her that she has an advantage over them. Her history with cancer will benefit her when it comes to placements and employment. Not that they minded her history when she displayed her scars in skin integrity class. Belinda would rather not have this advantage. Nor would her classmates if they thought about it. But we hope it does advantage you, Belinda. Because your history will bring so much to future patients. You navigated the medical system alone. You navigated support services alone. It will be easier for them – because of you.

HH

On My Own Two Feet

Matt was looking for love on a dating site and found it an altogether painful process. He'd establish a quick rapport online, but the chemistry in person eluded him. After a series of woeful first dates, Matt rolled the dice one last time, arranging a drink with a young lass by the name of Ellie Parker, telling himself if this girl wasn't the one, he would give up on the whole web-dating crusade and consign himself to the perils of chance.

Boy was she the one. Ellie matched her online persona, then some. She laughingly describes that first date as 'more like a job interview', but for Matt it was love at first sight. Ellie was initially reticent, but Matt earnt another encounter after two months of solid, almost charming harassment, and they've been joined at the hip ever since.

Matt and Ellie settled in Glenorchy, along the Derwent River just outside Hobart. Their first child, Harriette, was growing into a funny, deep and gentle human. Matt and Ellie's second child was on the way and, on paper, things couldn't have been going better. Harriette was flourishing. Ellie loved mumming and wifing. But, somewhat inconveniently, a black dog had made itself an unofficial tenant in Matt's head and began barking all sorts of nonsense. Matt couldn't give himself any credit for anything. He was ignoring things he did well and obsessing about things he got wrong. Everything was disproportionate. Matt merged towards a breakdown, driving between jobs was no longer a happy breather but time for the dog to snarl. He tried to dig himself out without telling anyone and was soon exposed as naive for thinking he was tough enough to get through on his own, which only perpetuated his sense of worthlessness. Matt couldn't avoid the truth of it. He had become the elephant in the room. The black dog and the fat elephant soon coalesced somehow, and Matt finally opened up to Ellie and dobbed on his brain. He cried and shook. Once he started talking about his fears, they shrank. That, coupled with Ellie's unwavering support, saw Matt emerge from his funk and begin to slowly rebuild.

Just two months later things went funny. Then weird. Then scary. Queen's Birthday long weekend, Sunday night. Matt left the dinner table to go to the bathroom and when he sat down on the toilet he felt like someone had suddenly hit him with full force on the side of the head with a sledgehammer. Thinking it was 'maybe a minor heart attack or something', Matt grabbed a couple of aspirin, went back to the dinner table with chronic pain now spilling from the side of his head down through his jaw, and mentioned to Ellie that he wasn't feeling well, but that the aspirins should do the trick. Later, as Matt was trying to get Harriette to bed, another wave of crippling nausea and pain shot through his body. Matt tried to tell Ellie that he was getting worse but he couldn't remember if he'd spoken the words aloud. Ellie assured Matt that she had heard him, that he had spoken the words. Matt's vision went kaleidoscopic as he was trying to text a couple of his doctor friends, then Ellie took over. She helped Matt to the car, grabbed Harriette and dropped her at Granma's, then rushed her fella to Emergency. They ran a bunch of tests but couldn't find anything, so they sent him home with some powerful migraine meds and told him to return if his condition worsened.

Almost a fortnight later, after a myriad of appointments and exhausting, inescapable pain, Matt flopped onto the couch one morning. They still had no idea what was wrong with him. He went out like a bulb. When he awoke, he felt very confused. Matt couldn't extricate himself from the blanket he lay under. He tried two or three times. He figured that the blanky must be tucked underneath him somehow. He'd really tucked himself in this time! After two more tries Matt realised that the tucking wasn't the issue. His left arm wasn't working, at all. Matt forced himself up with his right arm and fell straight onto the living-room floor because his left leg wouldn't work either. Trying not to panic, Matt looked around for his phone and spotted it at his feet, displaying a missed call from Ellie. So began ten solid minutes of 'flapping around like a stunned mullet in the bottom of a dinghy', trying to get to his phone to call Ellie back.

Ellie usually worked nine to five, but on this particular day, the local power company was cutting power to the street where her salon sat, so she finished by 11 a.m. Fortuitously, she was already on her way to him by the time Matt managed to finally call.

Matt vaguely remembers Ellie and the ambos leaning over his body on the floor. He felt like he was in a film. Matt was using all of his willpower just to stay conscious and focused. They told him he'd had a stroke. The damage was minimal *but* ... (Hearing a medic say 'but' is up there in scary-talk with a tradie saying 'oops'.) Matt passed out again, next thing he knew, the conversations were happening around him and out of earshot, he heard mention of Melbourne and wondered how he'd fathom the energy for a flight.

Matt spent his first days lying there and listening to the sounds of the ward. With barely a whisper to his voice it was a good chance to take stock. Pretty soon he started to feel lucky. Many of the people around him couldn't even name themselves and faced a long road to recovery. Matt was only thirty-eight. His relative youth was on his side. This time also afforded Matt plenty of time to think of all that had been done to keep him alive. The flights interstate. The world-class health care. Matt made a promise to himself from that hospital bed – whether he ever walked again or not – he was going to find a meaningful way to thank the countless people who had helped him to that point. He owed them that.

When Matt eventually returned home to Glenorchy in Tasmania, little Harriette had grown up considerably. She was very caring and supportive of Daddy, but also very strict with him. For quite a while, she insisted on accompanying him everywhere, even to the bathroom! She became quite the little supervisor.

When it comes to rehabbing the brain, Matt was told that the extent of his recovery would be determined by his attitude and adherence to the rehab program. As good a supervisor as his little Harriette was, Matt had no interest in maintaining her worry, and determined to commit himself fully to the recovery process.

There's a fine line between doing too little and going too hard when it comes to recovery from neurological events. Matt was keen to recover, but had to learn not to push too hard on his good days. It started with him leaning on Ellie to get to the bathroom. It ended with Matt signing up to do a 21-kilometre walk up a mountain for the National Stroke Foundation. Matt was pretty sure he couldn't do it all in one hit, and would be happy even if it meant twenty-one one-kilometre walks. He got the word out on social media and set an ambitious fundraising target. It was going well, before being supercharged when a chance interaction brought it to the attention of the Love Your Sister Village.

There's a group called 'The Hobart Mo Bros' – they're all serious runners, and every time there's a charity walk or run in Hobart, they bolt off at the starter's gun and always finish first. They form a guard of honour at the finish line, then enthusiastically cheer and whoop every single participant until the very last person has passed. They're famous in Hobart and they're known to be amongst the best ALOs (Atmosphere Liaison Officers) in the world.

You can imagine how Matt must've felt, coming in on his own two legs, from not being able to walk at all, to the

Mo Bros cheering and whooping like he was some kind of Olympian or something. Still on clouds, he found his fiancée Ellie, little Harriette and their new arrival, Eliott, at the after-party, then it all came home on him. The adrenaline held him aloft for two days.

Matt made the distance, raised $24 000 and became a poster boy for the National Stroke Foundation. He had found a way to say thanks to all who helped him. He repaid his debt.

As for his love, Ellie, he's thankful for her every day. For first giving him a reason to live. And for then giving him a reason to walk.

SJ

The VIP

Erin squared up to cancer ten years ago. It's a happy ending. She has been in remission for eight years and the memories of it are far behind her. Last year, she kept getting the dizzies. And felt a little tired. Turns out her heart wasn't up to the job. Pacemaker please. While she was in hospital after the surgery, she had glimpses of her first hurdle. A smell here, an image there and the memories came to the forefront. She decided she was in life's box seat. A VIP. She doesn't dwell on small disappointments or get caught up in materialism. She doesn't dismiss other people's feelings, and her radar for unintentionally hurting others is superior. She knows inherently that all that matters is each other. Our families, our friends, our communities. She loves throwing a party – bring your wallets because they're fundraisers too. She's writing her own book, to help others 'facing their mountains'. It's nearly finished.

Erin is thirteen years old.

HH

Acknowledgements

In the beginning, there was Max. I was sitting by a river where it met the sea watching the sun come up, when an old man with an even older dog walked by. The dog nuzzled me, I gave him a cuddle and within minutes I was sitting in Max's nearby donga having a cup of tea. There were bedraggled sepia photos of emus around the place, and Max waxed lyrical about the emu farm he had built after he retired as a builder. I learnt that girl emus select their mates by looking at the boy emus' butts – the bigger the better. When she lays her eggs, the boy sits on them while the girl goes out and finds the next best butt, has some more eggs and brings them back to the first boy's nest. She puts them in front of him one at a time and he pulls them in under himself and adds them to their growing brood. The conversation moved on to Max's family, and it turns out he was like a boy emu.

Back in the day he had found two kids sheltering in a house he was going to demolish, and he tracked down their father, who lived under a bridge with a suitcase full of mental health issues. Max arranged public housing for him, took the two kids in and blended them into his existing family – never denying them their father. After all the kids had kids, Max plucked out a troubled grandson, completed forty written units of a building course (a pesky new requirement to reregister as a builder) and took the boy on as an apprentice. The lad found a calling and left his wayward ways far behind. Max was eighty-five and said he'd been blessed with a wonderful life. I headed back to camp with a plump heart.

Sam had talked me into joining him on a Love Your Sister road trip to raise awareness and funds for cancer research. He explained that even though I'd been in the engine room of the charity for its duration, I had no idea what it was like out there fundraising, going to schools and attending community events. He was right.

Throughout our daily adventures, Max kept popping into my head and when we got back to camp, I wrote Max's story. I read it out to the road crew, and they were as transfixed as I had been about the amazing Max. An accidental tradition was born. Turned out there were Maxes everywhere. People doing extraordinary things. Going over and above. Finding time to make a difference. Doing something about 'it'; about all the 'its'. Between fundraisers, I'd seek out new everyday heroes and each night I'd tell tales about the wonderful things people were doing; how they'd turned adversity into triumph. These were special, magical times.

We started putting some stories on social media, which led to more and more stories. It wasn't just us seeing the magic; the people who read them saw it too. Together we laughed, we wept, we held our breath and cheered along as our everywhere heroes emerged. And it continued when we got home. Sam and I spent hours being inspired by your stories, and Sam suggested we make a book – a book about our heroes next door. Together. We melded our enthusiasm and belief in the magic of the human condition, and we embraced your lives, your actions, your stories. We hope you have been as touched and inspired by our heroes as we have been. That perhaps your life has been enriched by these tales too.

There are way more heroes than there are in this book and we want to thank everyone who mustered the courage to tell us about the deep selves in yourselves. And we are grateful to all the dobbers out there who told us about that special someone they knew. This was particularly helpful, because heroes don't always put up their hands; sometimes others need to toot their horns. Our lives are forever altered. You are all etched into our fabric. You are all our heroes next door.

If you could ask Santa for absolutely anything, what would you ask for? *Dear Santa* is a collection of letters to Santa from some of Australia's most notorious and best-loved grown-ups, including Helen Garner, Adam Hills, Deborah Mailman, Rove McManus, Leigh Sales, Grant Denyer and many more. Surprising, entertaining, wicked and witty, this little book of letters is the perfect gift for your favourite human.

If you could tell your dad anything, what would it be? *Dear Dad* is an honest, moving, emotionally memorable collection of letters to their fathers from some of Australia's most notable notables, including Steve Waugh, Trent Dalton, Samuel Johnson, Kathy Lette, John Williamson, Susie Youssef, Michala Banas, Glenn Shorrock, Matilda Brown, Joel Creasey, Shannon Noll, Michelle Law, Ben Gillies, Hilde Hinton, and many more. This heartfelt, honest and very human book of letters will make you smile and make you cry. It is the perfect gift for the dad in your life.